"The prosperity gospel is a false gospel, and prosperity preachers are false prophets. This book is as clear as that—and persuasive—but it is even more. Jones and Woodbridge have written a simple, careful account of the new religion that is sweeping Asia, Africa, and the Americas. And they've provided a fair, biblical, and searching critique. I'm sad to say that this book is desperately needed; I'm thankful that it's now available."

Mark Dever, Senior Pastor, Capitol Hill Baptist Church, Washington, DC

"In a work that is long overdue, Drs. Jones and Woodbridge deal the prosperity gospel a fatal blow through their thorough research and irrefutable documentation. The authors, blending biblical theology with persuasive wit, create a rare blend that will appeal to both the layperson and theologian. Churches wrestling with the destructive doctrine of the prosperity gospel now have a staunch advocate and ready defense that clearly delineates God's will on such matters."

Emir Fethi Caner, President, Truett-McConnell College, and coauthor of *Unveiling Islam*

"The prosperity gospel is neither prosperous nor is it the gospel as defined by Scripture. Simply put, it is a false teaching and a dangerous heresy. This book, written by two superb biblical scholars, carefully and accurately investigates, critiques, and exposes the biblical and theological errors that pervade this movement. This is an important and valuable work. I pray for its wide distribution and reading."

Daniel L. Akin, President, Southeastern Baptist Theological Seminary

"In this book Jones and Woodbridge have given us the truth about the prosperity gospel. This brief survey is remarkably clear and concise, providing both the historical background and biblical critique of this movement. Their treatment is fair and balanced, penetrating to the heart, and it reveals the danger of the prosperity gospel. I highly recommend this well-written book."

Benjamin L. Merkle, Associate Professor, Southeastern Baptist Theological Seminary, and editor of the 40 Questions & Answers Series

"I praise God for the release of this book. It is a reliable resource for all who want to understand the destructive nature of the prosperity gospel movement. Jones and Woodbridge carefully point out [the prosperity movement's] major biblical errors and call attention to the presence of erroneous concepts found in prosperity theology. By exposing these errors, as well as interacting with some of the leading proponents of the prosperity movement, Jones and Woodbridge have provided a wonderful resource to hand to those who've bought into a counterfeit gospel, and for pastors who desire to protect their flock from wolves. May God use this book to direct people to the only true gospel, and to the Savior, who is Himself our inheritance and our treasure."

Tony Merida, Teaching Pastor, Temple Baptist Church, and author of *Faithful Preaching* and *Orphanology*

"A great, balanced approach that is both biblically rigorous and in touch with current issues. An invaluable resource for those wishing to deal with this subject with accuracy and clarity. Very gospel-centered."

J. D. Greear, Lead Pastor, The Summit Church, and author of *Breaking the Islamic Code*

Health, Wealth & Happiness

Health, Wealth & Happiness

Has the Prosperity Gospel Overshadowed the Gospel of Christ?

David W. Jones
Russell S. Woodbridge

Kregel
Publications

Health, Wealth & Happiness: Has the Prosperity Gospel Overshadowed the Gospel of Christ?

© 2011 David W. Jones and Russell S. Woodbridge

Published by Kregel Publications, a division of Kregel, Inc., P.O. Box 2607, Grand Rapids, MI 49501.

Library of Congress Cataloging-in-Publication Data
Jones, David W. (David Wayne), 1973–
    Health, wealth & happiness : has the prosperity gospel overshadowed the gospel of Christ? / David W. Jones & Russell S. Woodbridge.
        p. cm.
        Includes index.
    1. Faith movement (Hagin) 2. Wealth—Religious aspects—Christianity. 3. Wealth—Biblical teaching. I. Woodbridge, Russell S., 1967– II. Title. III. Title: Health, wealth, and happiness.
BR1643.5.J69   2011   261.8'5—dc22   2010041562

ISBN 978-0-8254-2930-9

Printed in the United States of America
12 13 14 15 / 5 4 3 2

In memory of my grandfather,

Gustave H. Swanson,

who first taught me about money.

—DWJ

To my father,

Rev. Russell D. Woodbridge,

a faithful pastor for more than forty years.

—RSW

Contents

Preface

This book truly is a collaborative effort between two authors, each of whom has longstanding interest, professional training, and vocational experience in ministry and finance. While each of us is responsible for writing certain sections of this text, both of our fingerprints are on every page. As you begin reading, we thought it would be helpful for us to give a bit of personal background, as well as some insight into why we wrote this book.

DAVID W. JONES'S STORY

One of the earliest lessons I can recall my mother teaching me is "Money doesn't grow on trees." Obviously, my mother didn't think I believed money sprouted from the forest; this was simply her way of wisely turning down my request for a candy bar or a new pack of baseball cards. While the idea of dollar bills falling from the trees seemed almost comical to me as a young boy, being told "no" is never fun. Over time, however, I came to embrace the Puritan work ethic that still pervades much of the New England culture. The ideas of hard work, saving, intentional giving, and frugality became cornerstones in my early view of finances, and I now find myself telling my own children, "Money doesn't grow on trees."

When I became a Christian as a young person, like many new converts, I viewed Christianity as an eternal life insurance policy—that is, I embraced the spiritual aspects of Christianity, but I did not fully grasp the material dimensions of the gospel. Eventually, however, I began to understand that Christianity is not simply about the fate of people's souls; rather, the gospel is the message that Jesus died on the cross and was resurrected in order to redeem, restore, and reconcile all of creation on humanity's behalf and for His own glory (see Rom. 8:18–25; 1 Cor. 15:1–28). Over time I saw that Christianity is a worldview that impacts all of life. I came to understand that the gospel impacts our wallets as well as our souls, and I realized that the view of economics I had learned as a boy was largely biblical. When I entered vocational Christian service as a young man, I purposed to make the material implications of the gospel an emphasis within my ministry.

While I surely had been exposed to the prosperity gospel earlier in my life, it was not until I began my seminary training that I grasped the size and influence of the prosperity gospel movement. I was amazed to find classmates and laypeople who viewed their relationship to God as a give-and-get transaction. They saw God as a kind of sugar daddy who existed to make them healthy, wealthy, and happy on account of service rendered. While God certainly does provide and care for His followers, prosperity theology is a corruption of His self-revelation, a distortion of His plan of redemption, and an idea that can ultimately lead to a reckless view of the material world.

My ministry path has included Bible college, seminary, pastoral ministry, and various forms of denominational service. My interest in academics and education, as well as my concern for the practical aspects of Christianity, eventually led to a PhD in theological studies with an emphasis in financial ethics. I currently serve at Southeastern Baptist Theological Seminary in Wake Forest, North Carolina, where I teach a variety of classes, including the courses "The Ethics of Wealth and Poverty" and "The Created Order and Environmental Ethics." My studies have afforded me the opportunity to become well acquainted with the practical and academic writings of prosperity gospel advocates, both historical and modern.

Early in my academic career, I published a brief article entitled "The Bankruptcy of the Prosperity Gospel" in a rather obscure theological journal.[1] It was an attempt to synthesize my objections to prosperity theology, as well as try to give some direction to those caught up in the movement. While I have published more than a dozen articles and books since—including topics from the ethics of taxation to the morality of usury—I continue to get more feedback about my little prosperity gospel article than anything else I have written. In light of such reaction, I have long wanted to write a book about the prosperity gospel that could be used in the church.

Some time ago my colleague and longtime friend Russ Woodbridge suggested that we co-author a short book to address the failings of the prosperity gospel, as well as give direction to disillusioned followers of prosperity theology. Knowing Russ's own publication in the field, as well as his ministry service and background in high finance, I knew we would be a good team for such a project. The book you now hold in your hands is the fruit of our collaboration. Whether you are a church leader or layperson, a follower or opponent of the prosperity gospel, an expert in the field or just an information seeker, I trust and pray that the Lord will use this book to further conform you to Christ's image.

RUSSELL S. WOODBRIDGE'S STORY

Like my co-author, I also grew up in New England. Throughout my upbringing, my parents encouraged me to work hard, to give, and to save. More importantly, they taught me about God and, as a young boy, I repented of my sin and trusted Christ. After graduating from college, I moved to New York City to work for a well-known investment bank on Wall Street. Two years later the bank transferred me to its office in Frankfurt, Germany, where I ended up trading stocks and options for a living. Due to unfortunate circumstances, such as losing millions of dollars, the bank fired some traders and promoted me and one of my colleagues. My gifted colleague charted a new course and I went along for the ride: we made millions for the bank the next year.

God granted me success in trading but I was not satisfied. Money never satisfies. During this period of success, God changed my desires, and I left a lucrative career behind and returned to the United States to attend seminary. I learned that the purpose of life is not about accumulated money, health, or a great career—it's about knowing God. This series of events helped form my view of biblical stewardship and success.

While in seminary I met Kevin, a man paralyzed from birth, and he told me his story about trying to get healed at a crusade. What I remember is how devastating this event was to his spiritual life. The false promises of the prosperity gospel crushed Kevin's spirit, and he spent years recovering. This was my first personal encounter with the teachings of the prosperity gospel.

After seminary I had the privilege of serving as pastor of a small church in North Carolina. When I discovered that several ladies in the church watched Joyce Meyer on television and read her books, I examined her core doctrines and teachings and found them to be erroneous. I am sure that the women in my church were not aware of everything that Joyce Meyer believed. Until this experience, I was unaware that the prosperity gospel was so influential in conservative, Bible-believing churches.

While I was teaching at Southeastern Baptist Theological Seminary, different churches asked me to preach. Whenever I mentioned Joel Osteen or some other prosperity teacher from the pulpit, people would come to me after the service to make comments. Occasionally they had questions about the prosperity gospel. More often, they told me they did not agree with the prosperity gospel but their friends and relatives listen to prosperity teachers and send them money. My sense was that these concerned Christians didn't always know what to say to their friends and family about such teachers.

My financial background and theological training have created opportunities for me to teach courses on personal finance at the seminary and college, at a Bible institute, and in churches. From this platform, I have been able to teach biblical truth about money and to critique prosperity theology.[2]

The prosperity gospel has tremendous appeal, and it is growing both in the United States and internationally. Millions of people follow famous prosperity teachers, and their souls are at stake. The deception of so many is a tragedy that I hope this book can help address.

I pray that you will find this book useful. Perhaps it will confirm what you already know, give you new information to share with friends captured by the prosperity gospel, or open your eyes to the truth and help you reject the prosperity gospel. Ultimately, I hope this book will encourage you to "seek the things that are above, where Christ is" (Col. 3:1).

Acknowledgments

A number of people encouraged us to write this book. Our wives, Dawn Jones and Ingrid Woodbridge, are our greatest encouragers. Without their love and sacrifices, as well as the patience of our children, this book would not be in your hands.

We are indebted to resources we have read on the topic of the prosperity gospel, as well as the numerous conversations we have had with students and colleagues over the years, yet several deserve mention for their special assistance, critiques, and editorial improvements. We would like to acknowledge James K. Dew and Russell D. Woodbridge, who reviewed several chapters for content; Billie Goodenough for reading the entire manuscript and finding our mistakes; Dawn Jones for thoroughly editing each chapter and conforming them to the Kregel style guide; and several others who looked over the manuscript and gave advice, including William Aleshire, Benjamin Merkle, Andrew Spencer, Carrie Pickelsimer, and Ingrid Woodbridge.

Special thanks to Jim Weaver of Kregel Publications for his interest in and encouragement to submit the proposal. His ideas and input have improved the book. We also thank the marketing and editorial team at Kregel, including Cat Hoort, Miranda Gardner, and Wendy Widder for their insightful counsel and contributions to the manuscript. We, of course, assume responsibility for the final form and contents of this volume.

We would also like to express gratitude to the administration of Southeastern Baptist Theological Seminary, who provided support, resources, and time that allowed us to complete this book.

Introduction

Cindy, an accountant in Florida, listened intently to the prosperity preachers on television.[1] She heard their message, "Be faithful in your giving and God will reward you financially." And she saw their message—that is, she could be financially successful just like the heralds of the prosperity gospel. Inspired by their message, as well as their example, Cindy sent money to the ministries of Joyce Meyer, Paula White, and Benny Hinn, hoping to be rewarded for her faithfulness. She waited and waited, but the financial reward never appeared. Like many others, she first thought that she did not have enough faith to receive God's financial blessing. Later she realized that the prosperity preachers' promises were just plain false. Instead of improving her economic situation, Cindy's dabbling with the prosperity gospel made her financial woes worse. She ended up having to borrow money to buy groceries. Today Cindy is understandably angry, bitter, and disillusioned.

Kevin is also disillusioned. Paralyzed from the waist down due to a congenital birth defect, Kevin wants to walk. When as a boy he heard that a faith healer was coming to Raleigh, North Carolina, he begged his parents to take him to the crusade. The message Kevin heard there was that if he had enough faith, he would be healed; but his hopes for healing were quickly dashed when ushers at the crusade prevented him from sitting near the front, despite his disabled condition. Although seated near the back of the auditorium, Kevin did not give up his hopes of being chosen for divine healing. During the invitation Kevin waved his hands at the ushers to get their attention, but to no avail—they overlooked him, a seemingly obvious candidate for healing. An advocate for the handicapped, Brian Darby observes that, like many others, Kevin's sense of euphoria came crashing down when the hoped-for healing did not occur.[2] Today, Kevin remains in his wheelchair, disappointed but alive—unlike others who have stopped medical treatments after being "healed" at a prosperity gospel crusade and, in rare cases, have died shortly thereafter.[3]

While these may be sensational examples of the influence (and failings) of the prosperity gospel, other less extreme examples abound. Evangelical churches are full of people who, perhaps unknowingly, regularly watch prosperity gospel teachers on television. Here is a common scenario: the polished, friendly, motivational preacher asks for money in order to support his ministry; in return, he promises prayer on the donors' behalf, as well as a financial blessing from God. The viewers then send money because they appreciate the positive teaching and could use a little bit more money to pay their bills. When an increase in income does not occur, however, consumers of the prosperity message often become self-critical, thinking that the failure rests in their own lack of faith, or they become disappointed and angry with God. Undoubtedly, this scenario is played out repeatedly as significant numbers of Christians are influenced by the prosperity gospel.

What happened? How did the modern church arrive at a place where otherwise orthodox Christians would come to view God as a way to achieve personal success and as a means to attain material prosperity? In pondering these questions, consider the words of renowned pastor Charles Spurgeon, who just over one hundred years ago spoke these words to the then-largest congregation in all Christendom, "I believe that it is anti-Christian and unholy for any Christian to live with the object of accumulating wealth. You will say, 'Are we not to strive all we can to get all the money we can?' You may do so. I cannot doubt but what, in so doing, you may do service to the cause of God. But what I said was that to live with the object of accumulating wealth is anti-Christian."[4]

Over the years, however, the message preached in some of the largest churches in the world has changed. A new gospel is being taught today. This new gospel is perplexing—it omits Jesus and neglects the cross. Instead of promising Christ, this gospel promises health and wealth, and offers advice such as: declare to yourself that everything that you touch will prosper, for, in the words of a leading prosperity gospel preacher, "There is a miracle in your mouth."[5] According to this new gospel, if believers repeat positive confessions, focus their thoughts, and generate enough faith, God will release blessings upon their lives. This new gospel claims that God desires and even promises that believers will live a healthy and financially prosperous life.

A new gospel is being taught today. This new gospel is perplexing—it omits Jesus and neglects the cross.

This is the core message of what is known as the prosperity gospel. This gospel has been given many names, such as the "name it and claim it" gospel, the "blab it and grab it" gospel, the "health and wealth" gospel, the "word of faith" movement, the "gospel of success," "positive confession theology," and, as this book will refer to it, the "prosperity gospel." No matter what name is used, the teaching is the same. This egocentric gospel teaches that God wants believers to be materially prosperous in the here-and-now. Robert Tilton, one of the prosperity gospel's most well-known spokesmen, writes, "I believe that it is the will of God for all to prosper because I see it in the Word [of God], not because it has worked mightily for someone else. I do not put my eyes on men, but on God who gives me the power to get wealth."[6]

Without question, the prosperity gospel continues to grow and influence Christians. Fifty of the largest two hundred sixty churches in the United States promote the prosperity gospel.[7] The pastors of some of the largest churches in America proclaim the prosperity gospel, including Kenneth Copeland, T. D. Jakes, Joel Osteen, Frederick Price, Creflo Dollar, Kenneth Hagin Jr., and Eddie Long. Through the Internet, television, and radio, the prosperity gospel reaches millions around the world every day. Joel Osteen's Web site notes that his television program is available in one hundred countries, while roughly one million people download his services each week. Likewise, Joyce Meyer claims that her television program, *Enjoying Everyday Life*, reaches two-thirds of the world through television and radio and has been translated into thirty-eight languages.[8]

Given its departure from the historical, orthodox message of the church, one would think that most Bible-believing Christians would reject the prosperity gospel. However, this is not the case. The prosperity gospel is spreading beyond the confines of the charismatic movement, where it has been traditionally strong, and is taking root in the larger evangelical church. A recent survey found that in the United States, 46 percent of self-proclaimed Christians agree with the idea that God will grant material riches to all believers who have enough faith.[9] Why is this so? The prosperity gospel has an appealing but fatal message: accept God and He will bless you—because you deserve it.

The appeal of this teaching crosses racial, gender, denominational, and international boundaries. The prosperity gospel is on the rise not only in the United States but also in Africa, South America, India, and Korea, among many other places. In 2006, the Pew Forum conducted an international survey of Pentecostals and other like-minded Christians. The results of this survey were staggering. In Nigeria, 96 percent of those who professed belief in God either completely agreed or mostly agreed that God will grant material riches if one has enough faith. Believers in the countries of India (82 percent) and Guatemala (71 percent) gave similar responses. Likewise, a significant number of those surveyed asserted their belief that God will grant good health and relief from sickness to believers who have enough faith. When the Pew Forum asked if faith in God was an important factor in people's economic success, roughly 90 percent of those who responded in Kenya, Nigeria, and South Africa said it was.[10]

What accounts for the success of the prosperity gospel? A *Christianity Today* article noted that this movement is sweeping Africa because "American lifestyles have led African believers to equate Christian faith with wealth."[11] Influenced by American affluence and prosperity, native preachers readily take up the message of the prosperity gospel.[12] Additionally, American prosperity teachers export their message on television networks such as the Trinity Broadcasting Network, one of the most watched religious stations in the world.

In the United States, the popularity of prosperity preachers has caught the attention of the media and the government. The prosperity gospel phenomenon has appeared in magazines such as *Time* and *Newsweek* and television programs such as *Larry King Live* and *60 Minutes*. To the media's credit, the reporters sense the hypocrisy of prosperity gospel teachers—that is, wealthy preachers making promises that do not materialize to followers. Wealth does, however, materialize for many of the prosperity gospel teachers. With many of the most popular prosperity gospel teachers flaunting their wealth on television, it is not surprising that the U.S. Senate Finance Committee is currently investigating six ministries—all of which promote prosperity theology—to ensure that there has not been a misuse of donations.[13]

One of the most popular preachers in America is Joel Osteen, a proponent of the prosperity gospel. His church, Lakewood Church in Houston, Texas, has a weekly attendance of approximately forty thousand, and he reaches millions more through his broadcasts. With the release of *Your Best Life Now* (2004), *Become a Better You* (2007), and *It's Your Time* (2009), Osteen has gained influence among Christians of all denominations and has found an audience for his teachings. Yet, while sincere and likeable, Osteen preaches the prosperity gospel. Osteen's message will be analyzed more thoroughly in chapter 3. For the time being, consider the following example from Osteen's most recent work,

> When you say of the Lord you are healthy, you are whole, you are free, you are blessed, you are prosperous—when you say it, God has promised He will do it. . . . If you are not sharing in His favor, you might want to watch your words. Here's the key: If you don't unleash your words in the right direction, if you don't call in favor, you will not experience those blessings. Nothing happens unless we speak. Release your faith with your words.[14]

GROWTH OF THE PROSPERITY GOSPEL

Despite its departure from the historic Christian message, the prosperity gospel continues to grow exponentially around the globe. As has been noted, generally speaking, this is due to the self-centered bent of the prosperity message. There are, however, at least seven specific additional reasons why the prosperity gospel continues to grow, both in America and abroad.

First, the prosperity gospel contains a grain of biblical truth, albeit a grain of truth that has been greatly distorted. Proponents of the prosperity gospel teach that God is love, that He has the power to bless, and that He is exceedingly gracious toward His creation. God is love, has the power to bless, and does graciously provide for His people; yet, God does not promise material prosperity for all people. Instead, God promises something far better—Himself.

Second, the prosperity gospel appeals to the natural human desire to be successful, healthy, and financially secure. These desires are not inherently sinful; yet, they can become sinful if they supplant one's desire for God. The problem, then, is not with health and wealth but with one's attitude toward such things. Whenever we place our security and trust in anything or anyone other than Jesus Christ, we become idolaters. In a sense, then, the prosperity gospel brings out the worst in a wayward heart struggling to find sufficiency in Christ.

Third, the prosperity gospel promises much and requires little, portraying Jesus as one who can help believers help themselves. Instead of portraying Jesus as the one who made possible humanity's reconciliation with God, prosperity preachers tend to portray Jesus as the solution to material wants. Within prosperity theology, Jesus more closely resembles a servant of humans than the sinless Son of God.

Fourth, many advocates of the prosperity gospel have cultivated a winsome personality and a polished presentation of their message. Given that many modern Christians value style over substance, prosperity advocates find the contemporary church to be fertile ground for their ministry. Yet, while prosperity teachers are good communicators who are skilled at motivational speaking, their message must be compared to the Bible in order to validate their truth claims.

Fifth, many followers of the prosperity gospel have little knowledge of biblical doctrine. Therefore, they are ripe for accepting the distorted teachings of prosperity preachers. This is especially true given the Christian veneer of the prosperity message, which makes it attractive to listeners who may lack theological discernment. Christians must keep in mind that the biblical gospel is not Jesus plus material prosperity. As nineteenth-century pastor J. C. Ryle noted, "You may spoil the Gospel by substitution. You have only to withdraw from the eyes of the sinner the grand object which the Bible proposes to faith—Jesus Christ; and to substitute another object in His place. . . . Substitute anything for Christ, and the Gospel is totally spoiled! . . . You may spoil the Gospel by addition. You have only to add to Christ, the grand object of faith, some other objects as equally worthy of honor, and the mischief is done. Add anything to Christ, and the Gospel ceases to be a pure Gospel!"[15]

Sixth, many people have experienced success and healing (or at least claimed to have done so) and attribute it to the teachings of the prosperity gospel, thus "validating" its message. Modern Christians tend to be pragmatic in nature and incorrectly conclude that if a method works, it must be legitimate. People watch multimillionaire pastors on television tell their stories about how they believed a better day was coming and see that the pastors now have immense wealth. Hearing the powerful testimonies and having a pragmatic outlook, many Christians are understandably susceptible to the teachings of the prosperity gospel.

Seventh, many in the modern church lack a general sense of discernment because they are more influenced by the secular culture than by Scripture. Consequently, Christians often define happiness, joy, and success by the world's standards instead of using God's standards. Christians view success in terms of status, wealth, and position rather than holiness, faithfulness, and obedience to God. Regrettably, all too often there is little difference between a Christian and a worldly definition of prosperity.

PREVIEW OF CONTENTS

We write from the perspective that, as theologian Millard J. Erickson writes, "Theology is important because correct doctrinal beliefs are essential to the relationship between the believer and God."[16] A corollary to this statement is that an incorrect theology will lead to incorrect beliefs about God, His Word, and His dealings with humanity. Most importantly, the gospel must be rightly proclaimed because it is a matter of life and death for those who do not believe. Teaching or trusting in a false gospel has eternal ramifications. We know, as Paul writes, "The time is coming when people will not endure sound teaching, but having itching ears they will accumulate for themselves teachers to suit their own passions, and will turn away from listening to the truth and wander off into myths" (2 Tim. 4:3–4). It is a tragedy that many modern Christians are turning to a gospel of materialism to satisfy their souls, rather than to the gospel of Jesus Christ, the only hope for humankind.

You may feel uneasy when a loved one becomes enamored with the prosperity gospel or financially supports these ministries, though you may not know why you feel this way. Perhaps you need to know more about the prosperity gospel to articulate your concerns. We want to inform you about the prosperity gospel movement and equip you to help those who have let the prosperity gospel replace the gospel of Christ.

The first chapter begins with a survey of the historical foundations of the prosperity gospel. Few people realize that the prosperity gospel has its philosophical roots in a nineteenth-century movement known as New Thought. This movement, in some ways, is a forerunner to the modern New Age movement, as it rejects the orthodox teachings of Christianity in favor of a self-generated type of mysticism. The unorthodox teachings of the New Thought movement will be summarized using five categorical pillars. What will become clear as this chapter unfolds is that New Thought influenced the early proponents of the prosperity gospel.

Building on the survey of New Thought, chapter 2 provides a brief history of the prosperity gospel and its connection to New Thought. This is followed by a summary of the teachings of the prosperity gospel. Although prosperity teachers claim that their message is found in Scripture, there is little proof to substantiate this claim. As will become clear, the prosperity gospel has more in common with New Thought than with the New Testament. This chapter will explore the prosperity gospel's teachings about God, the mind, humankind, health and wealth, and salvation.

Chapter 3 examines some of the doctrinal errors of the prosperity gospel. While some Christians know that there are practical problems with the prosperity gospel, many do not realize the extent of the theological errors that underpin this movement. The chapter begins by defining the gospel according to Scripture before examining the prosperity teachings on a number of important theological doctrines, including faith, the atonement, the Abrahamic covenant, prayer, and the Bible. As will be shown, when we rightly understand the biblical gospel, it becomes obvious that the prosperity gospel cannot possibly be true.

Chapter 4 focuses on the important topic of suffering. The prosperity gospel has little to say about suffering—other than that Christians are not supposed to suffer, unless they lack faith or fail to make proper professions, speaking the right words. In light of the skewed view of suffering within prosperity theology, and the questions that are raised therein, this chapter covers a number of important biblical teachings on suffering, before developing a theology of suffering for Christians. Contrary to the teaching of the prosperity gospel, Christians do suffer and God has the ability to use such suffering for His purposes.

Chapter 5 builds a biblical theology of wealth and poverty. Whereas the prosperity gospel argues that faith is the key to material prosperity, the biblical message is that labor is a means of stewarding the created order. Whereas the prosperity gospel focuses on the furtherance of one's own finances, the Bible encourages believers to be concerned with the economic well-being of others. Whereas the prosperity gospel is fixated on the blessings of material goods, Scripture warns about the dangers of accumulating wealth. These and other areas of biblical teaching on wealth and poverty are explored in this chapter.

Finally, chapter 6 focuses on the topic of giving. It asks questions such as "Why should Christians give?" "How much should Christians give?" and "To whom should Christians give?" By looking at the biblical

teaching on benevolence, we hope that questions that arise related to giving are answered. While this book will not answer every question that
can be asked about the prosperity gospel, we trust that it will serve as an
appropriate introduction and that it will show many the bankruptcy of
the prosperity gospel.

PART 1

CRITIQUE

Chapter 1

The Foundations of the Prosperity Gospel

It was the top of the ninth inning, with two outs and nobody on base. The no-hitter was almost complete. The veteran Boston Red Sox pitcher, Curt Schilling, leaned toward home plate looking for his catcher's sign while the crowd cheered. The Boston catcher, Jason Varitek, called for a slider, down and away because he thought that the Oakland A's hitter Shannon Stewart would swing at the first pitch.

Schilling disagreed and waited until Varitek scrolled though the signs, his index finger finally pointing straight down toward the dirt, the universal sign for a fastball. Schilling reared back and delivered a 93-mile-per-hour fastball that Stewart smacked into right field for a clean single. After the game, Schilling said, "We get two outs, and I was sure, and I had a plan, and I shook Tek off and I get a big 'What if?' for the rest of my life."[1] Later, when Schilling reviewed the game, he admitted that he did not consider the immediate history of the game before throwing his pitch to Stewart. If he had, he would not have thrown a fastball in that situation, for it was too obvious of a pitch. For the entire game, Schilling had been throwing first-pitch fastballs to Stewart, so the fastball was the exact pitch that Stewart was expecting. Schilling's failure to consider the history of the game led to his fall—it cost him his last chance at throwing a no-hitter, a feat that only occurs on average twice per baseball season.

In all areas of life, failure to consider history can have profound implications for the present and the future.

While history can help determine the right pitch in a baseball game, it is far more important for interpreting Scripture, for formulating doctrine, and even for detecting false teaching. Unfortunately, many Christians are ignorant when it comes to history, even though Scripture encourages us to remember the past. While he was wrong in much of his analysis and counsel, Bildad wisely exhorts his friend Job, "For inquire, please, of bygone ages, and consider what the fathers have searched out. For we are but of yesterday and know nothing, for our days on earth are a shadow. Will they not teach you and tell you and utter words out of their understanding?" (Job 8:8–10). History can be a source of instruction and wisdom for the Christian.

Besides the biblical encouragement to remember the past, there are several other reasons to study history. First, Christianity is an inherently historical faith, based on supernatural acts in history and on the person of history, Jesus Christ. The Old Testament is the story of God, His chosen nation Israel, and the coming Messiah. In the New Testament, the Gospels and the book of Acts are primarily historical books that tell about supernatural acts related to the person of Jesus: His virgin birth; sinless life; sacrificial death on the cross; and glorious, bodily resurrection from the dead. The Scriptures, both Old and New Testaments, reveal God working out His purposes in history.

Second, history assists in interpreting Scripture and forming doctrine. When we study what earlier Christians believed, we can learn from their formulations of doctrine. When it comes to doctrine, newer is not always—or even usually—better. It is encouraging when we realize that our core beliefs are not new; early Christians formulated these same beliefs from Scripture. For example, the church councils of Nicaea (A.D. 325), Constantinople (A.D. 381), Ephesus (A.D. 431), and Chalcedon (A.D. 451) affirm the biblical teaching about God, the Trinity, the Holy Spirit, and Jesus being both fully man and fully God.

Third, history helps us assess our practices and interactions with the culture. Without an understanding of church history and a solid theological foundation, we lack perspective and the ability to assess current trends in our culture and are, as C. S. Lewis notes, enslaved to the recent past.[2] We cannot recognize false teachings or movements because we lack the historical perspective that can be gained by reading about our rich, theological heritage. Throughout history, novel ideas have given rise to movements that eventually faded but later reemerged in a new, slightly altered form. This, too, is true of the prosperity gospel.

The prosperity gospel is built upon a quasi-Christian heresy known as the New Thought movement, an ideology that gained popularity in the late nineteenth and early twentieth century.[3] Although the New Thought movement is unknown by name to most contemporary Christians, the prosperity gospel consists largely of the ideas of the New Thought movement repackaged with new faces, new technology, new venues, and a slightly altered message. While the prosperity gospel may look better than the classic New Thought movement, it still constitutes a departure from orthodox Christianity. Charles Spurgeon, the nineteenth-century English Baptist preacher, said it best, "A hog in a silk waist coat is still a hog."[4]

THE NEW THOUGHT MOVEMENT

The New Thought movement began in the nineteenth century and was known by several other names, including Mind-Cure, Mental Healing, or Harmonialism. In 1895, a New Thought group in Boston defined its purpose as "to promote interest in and the practice of a true philosophy and way of life and happiness; to show that through right thinking, one's loftiest ideals may be brought into present realization; and to advance intelligent and systematic treatment of disease by spiritual and mental methods."[5] While not a church or denomination, the New Thought movement was marked by religious beliefs not found in Scripture. Examples of such beliefs include that God is a force; spirit or mind is ultimate reality; people are divine; disease originates in the mind; and thoughts can create and/or change reality. Psychologist and philosopher William James commented in 1905 on New Thought's popularity, observing, "The mind-cure principles are beginning so to pervade the air that one catches their spirit at second-hand. One hears of the 'Gospel of Relaxation' of the 'Don't Worry Movement' of people who repeat to themselves 'Youth, health, vigor!' when dressing in the morning."[6] Furthermore, James noted that New Thought drew not only from the Gospels but also from Hinduism, philosophical idealism, transcendentalism, popular science evolution, and the optimistic spirit of progress. New Thought was a combination of pagan philosophies.

To understand the prosperity gospel's errors, we must first look at the beginnings of its historical predecessor, New Thought. Influential New Thought writers include Emanuel Swedenborg, Phineas Quimby, Ralph Waldo Trine, Norman Vincent Peale, Ernest Holmes, and Charles Fillmore. As we summarize the theology of these figures and, in the next chapter, compare New Thought beliefs with the teachings of the advocates of the prosperity gospel, it will be obvious that New Thought ideas permeate the prosperity gospel.

Emanuel Swedenborg: Grandfather of New Thought

Emanuel Swedenborg (1688–1772) was an important eighteenth-century Swedish scientist and inventor. He is known for his contributions in the fields of mathematics, astronomy, economics, political theory, and medicine; yet, his most significant and lasting contribution was in religion. In 1734 Swedenborg published a book entitled *The Infinite*, which was a study that summarized his search for the human soul. A decade later, still searching for the human soul, he reported that the Lord had appeared to him and told him to publish new doctrine for the church, which he did in his work entitled *Heavenly Secrets*. In this second book Swedenborg claimed for himself the title "The Unique Revealer of the Lord." In this capacity he claimed to have dialogued with the apostle Paul for a year, spoken several hundred times with the Reformer Martin Luther, and on at least one occasion had personal communication with Moses. Furthermore, he professed to be a clairvoyant who, over a period of twenty-seven years, possessed the power to look into heaven, hell, and other dimensions of the spirit world. While Swedenborg's claims of extrabiblical revelation alone raise questions about his orthodoxy, he also rejected orthodox Christian beliefs such as the doctrine of the Trinity, the deity of Jesus Christ, and salvation by grace through faith alone.

A review of Swedenborg's key works reveals that his doctrine included, among other things, belief in God as a mystical force, the notion that the human mind has the capacity to control the physical world, and the teaching of a works-based self-salvation scheme—ideas that later became core doctrines of New Thought. At the root of these teachings is the belief that the ultimate nature of reality is rooted in the nonphysical, the spiritual, or simply in the mind. For some philosophers, the physical world is simply an extension of the mind, and the mind or ideas constitute reality, not the material world.[7] Not surprisingly, in 1770 the Royal Council of Sweden condemned Swedenborg's doctrines, prompting him to relocate to Holland and eventually to England.

Unfortunately, though, many of Swedenborg's writings were distributed and widely read in America. Over time, his teachings influenced individuals such as Ralph Waldo Trine, Warren Felt Evans, and others who founded what became known as the New Thought movement. Martin Larson concludes his text *New Thought or a Modern Religious Approach* with an apt portrayal and observation of Swedenborg: "He is the grand fountainhead of a variety of deviationist religious movements; and specifically, the grandfather of New Thought."[8]

Phineas Quimby: Father of New Thought

Phineas Parkhurst Quimby (1802–1866), the intellectual father of New Thought, was a clockmaker by trade until he discovered the dubious art of mesmerism. This came about when Quimby met Lucius Burkmar, a man who seemed to have clairvoyant powers when hypnotized. When under hypnosis, Burkmar appeared to have the ability to accurately diagnose patients with various diseases. Observing this phenomenon led Quimby to pioneer and develop the idea of mental healing.[9] The basis for Quimby's theory was the idea that the mind possesses the ability to create and influence. For example, Quimby claimed that he could cause a person to stop walking simply by thinking or visualizing that situation.

Eventually, Quimby claimed to have developed his own clairvoyant powers and became a successful hypnotist.[10]

If I believe I am sick, I am sick, for my feelings are my sickness, and my sickness is my belief, and my belief is my mind. Therefore all disease is in the mind or belief.
Phineas Parkhurst Quimby

Quimby believed that sickness follows a disturbance of the mind; therefore, disease is really mental and the cure is to correct false reasoning or error in the mind. Quimby asserts, "If I believe I am sick, I am sick, for my feelings are my sickness, and my sickness is my belief, and my belief is my mind. Therefore all disease is in the mind or belief."[11] Quimby's philosophy, then, was whatever one believes is reality, including illness. In a summary of the essential elements of New Thought, Simon Coleman observes, "True reality was seen as being created on a spiritual level prior to its manifestation in physical realms."[12] Like Swedenborg, Quimby believed that the mind creates and controls reality. With this theory, Quimby helped establish the foundation for New Thought.

Quimby and other New Thought teachers placed little emphasis on the physical world. The idea that the mind is the ultimate power that shapes reality led Quimby to deny the bodily resurrection of Jesus. If the mind or spiritual is good and matter is evil, it makes little sense that Jesus would be resurrected with a physical body. Quimby also argued that Jesus was just another man who had superior ideas. In order to cure people, He simply changed their minds with His teachings—the same method that Quimby himself practiced. After all, the problem was the sick person's thinking patterns. Quimby's lasting influence came through his patients and students, who took his basic philosophy of mind-cure and developed it for their own purposes.

One of Quimby's patients and students was Warren Felt Evans (1817–1889), a member of a Swedenborgian church, who became a prolific writer for New Thought philosophy. His works included *Mental Cure, Mental Medicine,* and *Soul and Body.* Another Quimby patient, Mary Baker Eddy, wrote *Science and Health with Key to the Scripture,* published the newspaper *The Christian Science Monitor,* started Massachusetts Metaphysical College, founded the First Church of Christ, and birthed one of the largest Christian cults, known as Christian Science. Though not as influential as Eddy, Julius Dresser and his wife conducted healing classes based on Quimby's teachings and gave formal organization to New Thought. Starting in 1899, groups held New Thought conventions around the United States, and by 1914 the International New Thought Alliance was formed in order to serve all branches of New Thought followers, including groups such as Christian Science founded by Eddy and the Unity School of Christianity founded by Charles Fillmore.

Whatever may be said in praise of poverty, the fact remains that it is not possible to live a really complete or successful life unless one is rich.
Wallace D. Wattles

Ralph Waldo Trine: Evangelist of New Thought

In the earlier years of the twentieth century, numerous books began to appear that incorporated New Thought ideas with the aim of helping people achieve health and success. Examples include Ernest Holmes's *Creative Mind and Success,* Napoleon Hill's *Think and Grow Rich,* and Wallace D. Wattles's *The Science of Getting Rich,* which opens with, "Whatever may be said in praise of poverty, the fact remains that it is not possible to live a really complete or successful life unless one is rich."[13] In these New Thought works, one can discern some of the key recurring elements of the prosperity gospel: speaking the right words, invoking a universal law of success with words, and having faith in oneself.

Of all of the early twentieth-century New Thought writers, however, Ralph Waldo Trine (1866–1958) was the most prolific. Born in Illinois and educated at Knox College and the University of Wisconsin, Trine was responsible for popularizing New Thought ideas. American religious historian Sydney Ahlstrom calls Trine the "patriarch of the modern health and harmony tradition."[14] Trine's *In Tune with the Infinite: Fullness of Peace, Power and Plenty*, first published in 1897, sold millions of copies and was translated into over twenty languages. Charles Braden notes that Trine's book reached the general public, who bought the book without "ever knowing they were reading New Thought."[15] He argues that Trine's book is an "almost perfect presentation of New Thought at its best. . . . Where would one go for a better statement of the promise of New Thought?"[16]

Given that Trine's works were so popular, even among many professing Christians, it is important to ask what Trine believed about Christianity. Unfortunately, a survey of Trine's works reveals that his beliefs were far from orthodox.

First, Trine rejects the uniqueness of Scripture by claiming that Buddha's writings were also divinely inspired. Trine scolds Christians: "Your error is not in believing that your particular scriptures are inspired, but your error is—and you show your absurdly laughable limitations by it— your inability to see that other scriptures are also inspired."[17]

Second, Trine advocates theological pluralism—that is, he does not believe that faith in Jesus Christ, or any other particular savior, is the only means of salvation. Instead, he proposes that every religion leads to God. According to Trine, every religion is the same, and if you do not acknowledge this fact, then you are limiting yourself. He also believes all organized religions possess the truth that one must find unity with the Infinite. It does not matter what name you give to the Infinite, notes Trine, as long as you seek union with the Infinite. In Trine's system of belief, all that is needed for worship is a concept of God and a willing human soul.

Third, although Trine mentions Jesus throughout his works, he is more concerned with the moral teachings of Jesus than with the person and work of Jesus. In his best-selling book, *In Tune with the Infinite*, there is no mention of sin, repentance, or the gospel. According to Trine, such historic orthodox concepts are irrelevant, as the way to peace with God is to become conscious of oneness with the Father. When people come to this point, Trine believes, the force and the laws that govern the universe are within their powers because infinite intelligence and power can then work through them. For this power to work, however, their thoughts have to be illumined in order to provide intuition, an "inner spiritual sense through which man is opened to the direct revelation and knowledge of God, the secrets of life and nature."[18] According to Trine, such higher knowledge allows one to tap into universal laws and to achieve success in life. He describes this process as "condition[ing] your life in exact accord with what you would have it."[19]

Norman Vincent Peale: Pastor of New Thought

Despite the fact that Trine's ideas held little in common with biblical Christianity, his mystical, heretical teachings were read and accepted by people from all walks of life, including many orthodox believers. Yet, Trine was not the only writer to spread New Thought philosophy with success. Another well-known advocate of New Thought was Norman Vincent Peale (1898–1993), pastor of Marble Collegiate Church in New York City. He is best known for his book *The Power of Positive Thinking* (1952) that popularized New Thought ideas and techniques in America.[20] In *Guide to Confident Living*, Peale has chapters such as "Prayer—The Most Powerful Form of Energy," "How to Think Your Way to Success," and concludes his book with a chapter entitled "Change Your Thoughts and You Change Everything."[21] That Peale accepted and became an advocate of New Thought is surprising in light of the fact that his church was part of the Dutch Reformed Church, a historical, conservative, biblically rooted, Calvinistic denomination.

While the writings of Peale have more of a biblical veneer than the works of some other New Thought authors, it is clear that New Thought philosophy greatly influenced him. Peale readily admits that he read various metaphysical teachers, and he freely quotes them throughout his works, including Ernest Holmes (1887–1960) and Charles Fillmore (1854–1931), among other popular New Thought writers. In *The Tough-Minded Optimist*, Peale says that he regularly read the popular literature that poured into the homes of his congregants. This literature included material from the Unity Movement, Science of Mind, and Christian Science.[22] Peale suggests these writers taught that "Jesus Christ established a scientific, completely workable way of thought and life that brought about change and victory."[23] By his own admission, Peale was searching for a "practical and specific message for modern human beings that would really work when needed."[24] Although Peale claims to affirm the teachings of orthodox Christianity, his writings reflect a far more optimistic view of humankind than is presented in the Bible, thus demonstrating a significant problem with the prosperity gospel—it dangerously merges biblical ideas and secular thought.

THE PILLARS OF NEW THOUGHT PHILOSOPHY

In part because of the Christian veneer that it was often given, New Thought experienced success in America despite its nonbiblical roots. In this section, we will examine some core tenets of New Thought that had an impact on the prosperity gospel. These core beliefs can be summarized in five categorical pillars: (1) a distorted view of God, (2) an elevation of mind over matter, (3) an exalted view of humankind, (4) a focus on health and wealth, and (5) an unorthodox view of salvation.

Pillar One: A Distorted View of God

While not all New Thought writers have the exact same view of God, it is certain that the general teachings about God within New Thought philosophy diverge from the biblical doctrine of God. The gap between New Thought ideas about God and the scriptural view of God can be highlighted with three observations. First, most New Thought teachers reject the historic, orthodox, Christian doctrine of the Trinity. Instead, they embrace God in His oneness and deny that God is three distinct persons simultaneously. Second, many New Thought advocates propose that God and the world are of one substance or that the world is simply an extension of God. These ideas are respectively known as pantheism and panentheism, both of which diverge from a Christian worldview. Third, and most common among New Thought proponents, is the idea that God is an impersonal life-force or creative energy that must be harnessed in order to be successful.

Obviously, none of these claims reflect biblical teaching. Concerning the Trinity, the Bible teaches that God is one in His essence, yet He exists eternally and equally in three distinct persons: God the Father, God the Son, and God the Holy Spirit. Many New Thought proponents were Unitarians, including Mary Baker Eddy (1821–1910), founder of Christian Science; Charles Emerson (1837–1908), president of Emerson College; and Charles Fillmore, founder of the Unity School of Christianity. They believed that God is a single personality or that God simply reveals Himself in three different modes—first as the Father, then as the Son, and finally as the Spirit—but that He is not all three persons simultaneously. This is an ancient heresy known as modalism, and early church councils repeatedly condemned it.

For both Unitarians and New Thought teachers, Jesus was merely a prophet, perhaps divine and probably supernatural, but certainly not God. Charles Fillmore, in his book *Prosperity*, states, "We believe that Jesus expressed his divine potential and sought to show humankind how to express ours as well. We see Jesus as a master teacher of universal truths and as our Way Shower. In Unity, we use the term *Christ* to mean the divinity in humankind. Jesus is the great example of the Christ in expression."[25] This is a remarkable conclusion since Jesus says, "I and the Father are one" (John 10:30). The Gospel narratives also report that God the Father, God the Son, and God the Holy Spirit were all present simultaneously at Jesus' baptism (Matt. 3:16–17; Luke 3:21–22).

Concerning the proper relationship between God and the world, the Bible teaches that the triune God is the Creator of heaven and earth (Gen. 1:1). Prior to creation, only the triune God existed. When God spoke, He created this world out of nothing and thus the world had a beginning. Since God did not create the world out of Himself, He is distinct and separate from the created order. The Bible teaches that God is eternal and perfect and does not depend upon the world to complete His nature. In *Divine Providence* Emanuel Swedenborg opposes the biblical teaching that God created the world out of nothing, instead asserting that God is to be identified with all substance in the world.[26] Swedenborg even teaches that God ought to be equated with the physical sun of the present universe.[27]

Swedenborg is just one of many New Thought teachers who distort biblical teaching. In *Creative Mind and Success*, Ernest Holmes responds to the question "How does everything come into being?" by answering, "God makes them out of Himself. God thinks, or knows, and that thing which He thinks or knows appears from Himself, and is made out of Himself. There is no other possible explanation for what we see."[28] Ralph Waldo Trine, who was influenced by Swedenborg's writings, similarly refers to God as "the Spirit of Infinite Life and Power that is [in] back of all, that animates all, that manifests itself in and through all."[29] This view of God is known as pantheism, a heretical position. If God is identical to the world, then perhaps people should worship creation because it is divine. In fact, since human beings are part of the world, perhaps the individual should worship him- or herself as god. In the January 1907 edition of *Unity* magazine, a reader reaches this conclusion, yet wonders why human beings make mistakes if we are gods. New Thought proponent Jennie Croft answers, "God is all, in the sense that God is the great Energy or Force which is the source and cause of all that is. . . . Error does not arise with God; the error is in man's lack of knowledge of this beneficent Force dwelling within him."[30] The key, then, is to tap into this secret knowledge in order to be successful and to prevent mistakes.

These teachings about God's relationship to the world more closely reflect the concept of God in Hinduism than the biblical doctrine of God. Wallace Wattles, author of *The Science of Getting Rich*, freely admits this when he writes, "The monistic theory of the universe, the theory that is One is All and that All is One; that one Substance manifests itself as the seeming many elements of the material world is of Hindu origin."[31] Wattles encourages the reader to investigate further this philosophical view since it is the foundation for his New Thought book.

Since New Thought believes that the world emanates from God and that every created thing is part of God to some degree, it is not surprising that New Thought conceives of God as an impersonal force, substance, creative energy, Infinite Spirit, or Life Giver. Supposedly, this beneficent force is present throughout the universe and establishes universal laws that govern life. These universal laws dictate that there is a force or energy that fills the universe and must be absorbed in order for one to become prosperous and healthy. Swedenborg calls this idea his doctrine of "divine influx." He believes that God is a universal source from whom a "vitalizing power flows constantly and universally from the central life-giving force into everything that exists."[32] If a person wants to live fully, then he "needs only open the sluice-gates of his mind-soul to allow this natural force to flow in and possess him."[33]

Within the New Thought system, once people allow the omnipresent force of the Infinite to enter their minds, they discover the universal laws that govern the world. The task of the New Thought believer, then, is to harness the universal laws already present for humanity's benefit. These laws or ideas define reality; yet, if ideas are ultimate reality, then the material world is a malleable illusion. Hence, at the conclusion of *Prosperity*, Charles Fillmore contends, "In the following lessons we have attempted to explain man's lawful appropriation of the supplies spiritually and electrically provided by God. . . . Let us explain that all creative processes involve a realm of ideas and a realm of patterns or expressions of those ideas. The patterns arrest or 'bottle up' the free electric units that sustain the visible thing."[34] He explains further that electrical thought forms will transform these ideas into cosmic rays that crystallize into earthly things.[35]

In summary, New Thought distorts the biblical doctrine of God by turning God into an impersonal force or energy field. With its deficient view of God's creation, New Thought misconstrues the nature of reality and makes the mind or thoughts the key to controlling and creating the future. Ultimately, then, the objective of New Thought is to tap into the universal ideas or cosmic forces. How this feat is accomplished is the subject of the next categorical pillar.

Pillar Two: An Elevation of Mind over Matter

New Thought argues that harnessing one's mind or thoughts is the key to being successful. New Thought defines thoughts as forces that can and do create reality. As a person opens up to the divine influx and begins to recognize the universal laws, thoughts can then be focused with the aim of bringing about a desired state of affairs. According to New Thought advocates, this is the great secret of life—that is, if you think a certain way, then you can change reality. This is so because thoughts, spirit, and mind are what are real, while the physical world is an illusion. In other words, your mind is far more important than matter.

Since the mind is the key to success, New Thought writers stress the role of the mind and its mystical powers. For example, Charles Fillmore writes, "The Father has provided a universal seed substance that responds with magical power to the active mind of man."[36] Trine concurs: "Ideas have occult power, and ideas, when rightly planted and rightly tended, are the seeds that actualize material conditions."[37] The International New Thought Alliance declares, "We affirm that our mental states are carried forward into manifestation and become our experience in daily living."[38] According to New Thought, you possess the power in your mind to dictate to the world what you desire. Napoleon Hill (1883–1970) promises in his book *Success Through A Positive Mental Attitude* (1960), "You are a mind with a body! Because you are a mind, you possess mystical powers—powers known and unknown. . . . When you make the discoveries that are awaiting you, they can bring you: (1) physical, mental, and moral health, happiness, and wealth; (2) success in your chosen field of endeavor; and even (3) a means to affect, use, control, or harmonize with powers known and unknown."[39]

In a somewhat bizarre explanation of how people acquire this power and what it is made of, Napoleon Hill writes in *Think and Grow Rich* (1938), "Energy is Nature's universal set of building blocks, out of which she constructs every material thing in the universe, including man, and every form of animal and vegetable life. Through a process which only Nature completely understands, she translates energy into matter. Nature's building blocks are available to man, in the energy involved in thinking! Man's brain may be compared to an electric battery. It absorbs energy from the ether, which permeates every atom of matter, and fills the entire universe."[40]

According to New Thought, then, the key to success is to think the right thoughts because they dictate the outcome of one's situation. The reason people are not successful or healthy is because they have negative thoughts. They are not in tune with the universal laws or supernatural forces that are available to humankind. As Trine explains, "Send out your thought—thought is a force, and it has occult power of unknown proportions when rightly used and wisely directed—send out your thought that the right situation or the right work will come to you at the right time, in the right way, and that you will recognize it when it comes."[41] Note how Trine, like Charles Fillmore, explicitly mentions the occultist nature of thoughts or ideas and promises complete success if one uses such thoughts properly.

He who lives in the realization of his oneness with this Infinite Power becomes a magnet to attract to himself a continual supply of whatsoever things he desires.
Ralph Waldo Trine

New Thought teachers believe that there are laws in operation in the universe, particularly the law of attraction, the idea that people attract whatever they think. If humans can become one with the Infinite, understand the laws and focus their thoughts, then good things will happen. As Trine explains, "He who lives in the realization of his oneness with this Infinite Power becomes a magnet to attract to himself a continual supply of whatsoever things he desires. . . . If you have the thought of poverty, you will be poor, but if you entertain thoughts of prosperity, you set into operation forces that will bring about prosperous conditions."[42]

Again, within the New Thought system, the power to succeed is inside each person. It only has to be directed toward positive thoughts and success will become a reality. Ernest Holmes captures this sentiment when he writes, "We will always attract to us, in our lives and conditions, according to our thought. Things are but outer manifestations of inner mental concepts. Thought is not only power; it is the form of all things. The conditions that we attract will correspond exactly to our mental pictures."[43] In other words, visualize what you want and meditate upon that picture, and you will create it in reality.

Another New Thought writer, Charles Haanel, develops an entire plan for living on the so-called law of attraction. He explains his concepts in a lengthy text that he entitled, *The Master Key System*. In his volume Haanel writes, "If you require [i.e., consider] wealth a realization of the fact that the 'I' in you is one with the Universal mind which is all substance, and is Omnipotent, [this] will assist you in bringing into operation the law of attraction which will bring you into vibration with those forces which make for success and bring about conditions of power and affluence in direct proportion with the character and purpose of your affirmation."[44]

New Thought advocates teach that the mind—a properly oriented thought life—is the key to tapping into the divine power that is present throughout the universe. By implementing this process, which by default exalts humanity and demotes God, humans have the power to get whatever they desire—namely, success and prosperity in all realms of life. According to New Thought, the truth of mind over matter is the secret to controlling one's life and even changing the future. The potential powers that New Thought prescribes for a person make him or her somewhat godlike.

Pillar Three: An Exalted View of Humankind

New Thought literature reveals a human-centered philosophy that asserts that people are intrinsically good, spiritual beings, with the potential for godlike—if not divine—status. As people harmonize with the divine energy or Infinite Spirit through properly oriented thought, they become conduits for good works. The International New Thought Alliance claims, "We affirm the unity of God and humanity, in that the divine nature dwells within and expresses through each of us, by means of our acceptance of it . . . health, supply, wisdom, love, life, truth, power, beauty, and peace."[45] Such acceptance of the divine nature is defined as a mystical consciousness of being one with God, the life-force and power.

In New Thought terminology, people must open themselves to the divine influx. Through this encounter, a person not only becomes one with God but also becomes godlike. Within the New Thought framework, there is little to distinguish humans from the Creator. Trine summarizes, "The great central fact in human life, in your life and in mine, is the coming into conscious, vital realization of our oneness with this Infinite Life, and the opening of ourselves fully to this divine inflow. . . . In the degree that we open ourselves to this divine inflow are we changed from mere men into God-men."[46] He continues, "In essence the life of God and the life of man are identically the same, and so are one. They differ not in essence, in quality; they differ in degree."[47] Trine further reminds his readers that it takes a god to recognize a God.

According to New Thought, as long as a person continues to harness the divine power and universal laws, as a god he or she can become prosperous. The International New Thought Alliance affirms, "We are all spiritual beings, dwelling in a spiritual universe that is governed by spiritual law. . . . In alignment with spiritual law, we can heal, prosper, and harmonize."[48] The key to success is to recognize that you are a spiritual being who is able to tap into the spiritual laws that govern the universe.

Of course, in light of the teaching that humans can become gods, there is no mention of sin and redemption within New Thought. Since proponents of this philosophy neither acknowledge the deity of Jesus nor the inherent sinfulness of humanity, redemption is both impossible and unnecessary. As New Thought advocate Ernest Holmes writes, "Jesus was not God. He was the manifestation of God; and so are all people. 'I say that ye are gods, and every one of you sons of [the] Most High.'"[49]

Warren Felt Evans, an early New Thought writer and believer in the deification of man, purposefully avoids a discussion of Christ's incarnation, death, burial, and resurrection for the purpose of redeeming fallen humanity. Instead, Evans asserts that Jesus came to earth "so that every man might walk forth consciously to himself as a son of God and say, 'I and my Father are one.' . . . Then will be fulfilled the dream of Oriental Philosophy, which has haunted the Eastern mind from the remotest ages. 'The idea of God's becoming man . . . and man becoming God, is the mystic circle in which all their thoughts revolve. . . . Somehow, God and man, the infinite and finite, must become one.'"[50]

If people are essentially gods, then what kind of redemption do they really need? In New Thought there is no place for a sinless Savior who died on the cross in order to make propitiation for sin. Humans can save themselves from their dire circumstances through using the divine energy in the universe. They are, after all, in control of their fate. Ernest Holmes captures this belief when he writes, "If we partake of the divine nature we must know the same thing in our lives that God knows in His. 'I am master of my fate, I am the captain of my soul.' . . . Know that you cannot get away from this One Mind; that wherever you may go, there, right beside you, waiting to be used, is all the power there is in the whole universe. When you realize this you will know that in union with this, the only power, you are more than all else."[51]

New Thought's belief in the deification of humans is consistent with its belief that all is one and one is all. If all of creation is part of God or an extension of God, then people must be divine. To be clear, New Thought does not teach that people are divine as the result of the indwelling of the Holy Spirit or as the result of being made in the image of God. The movement holds that God is not distinct from creation and is an impersonal substance that gives life and energy to all reality. There is no distinction between God and people. If one achieves unity with the god-force through a proper orientation of thoughts, health and wealth are available for the taking.

Pillar Four: A Focus on Health and Wealth

New Thought believes that God is an impersonal life-force, that the mind controls matter, and that people are (or can at least become) gods. By way of practical application, since the human mind is all-powerful, this means that thoughts play a vital role in both permitting and removing bodily diseases, as well as greatly affecting the achievement of financial success.

Considering health first, according to New Thought, if one is properly connected to the Infinite, sickness should not be manifest. How does a person, especially a follower of New Thought, become ill in the first place? Trine responds, "For very clearly, the life of this Infinite Spirit, from its very nature, can admit no disease; and if this is true, no disease can exist in the body where it freely enters, through which it freely flows."[52] If the Infinite Spirit cannot admit disease into the body, then the culprit must be your mind; you broke a universal law whether you intended to or not. Promoting the power of words, Trine continues, "Never affirm or repeat about your health what you do not wish to be true. Do not dwell upon your ailments, nor study your symptoms. Never allow yourself to be convinced that you are not complete master of yourself. Stoutly affirm your superiority over bodily ills, and do not acknowledge yourself the slave of any inferior power."[53]

New Thought proposes that people become sick because of negative thoughts or on account of the fact that they are not properly attuned to the Infinite. People allow disease to enter their bodies, thus giving disease its power. The solution to illness is to think about being healthy and have faith that the law of attraction will work. In other words, the cure for disease is simply an application of mind over matter. Quimby asserts, "All disease is in the mind or belief. Now as our belief or disease is made up of ideas, which are [spiritual] matter, it is necessary to know what beliefs we are in; for to cure the disease is to correct the error, and as disease is what follows the error, destroy the cause, and the effect will cease. How can this be done? By a knowledge of harmony."[54]

Likewise, New Thought writer Thomas Troward claims in his book *The Law and the Word* that through an impersonal cosmic soul, we can "send out our Thought for the healing of disease, for the suggestion of good and happy ideas, and for many other beneficial ideas."[55] In *Dynamic Thought*, Henry Hamblin echoes this idea of harnessing what he called the Divine Mind to heal: "In healing the sick it is not necessary to see them or go near them, you may be hundreds of miles away and it will make no difference, for we are all in God (Divine Mind) and God is in us, and we all form one complete whole."[56]

Not surprisingly, this teaching of mind healing can be traced back to the grandfather of New Thought, Emanuel Swedenborg, who equates disease with ignorance. Swedenborg writes, "Sickness is simply a malady which, because of sin or error or a failure of understanding, attacks the temporary or unreal man; the spiritual man can have no cognizance of disease."[57] People are spirits or minds trapped in physical bodies. Since reality is the mind, nothing can invade or attack people unless there is something wrong with their thinking.

By way of contemporary application, think about how devastating this philosophy can be to someone with cancer. According to New Thought, you are the reason you have cancer. You are at fault. You must have done something or thought something to attract the cancer to your body. The cure is not found by going to the doctor's office; rather, it is in your mind. Change your thoughts and the cancer will be removed. If the cancer advances, then once again, you are the problem. You did not think the right thoughts or believe in the universal laws or harness the divine influx. Perhaps you did not have enough faith in the universal laws. In New Thought, there is absolutely no consideration of God, His providence, or His purposes in human suffering and sickness.

New Thought promises not only good health with right thinking but also financial prosperity and personal success. Whether the topic is related to health or wealth, the method is the same: control thoughts and success will materialize. Visualize and meditate about wealth and eventually prosperity will come. According to Wattles, people deserve wealth as it is their right. In the opening to his book, *The Science of Getting Rich*, he says,

> Whatever may be said in praise of poverty, the fact remains that it is not possible to live a really complete or successful life unless one is rich. No man can rise to his greatest possible height in talent or soul development unless he has plenty of money; for to unfold the soul and to develop talent he must have many things to use, and

he cannot have these things unless he has money to buy them. . . . Man's right to life means his right to have the free and unrestricted use of all the things which may be necessary to his fullest mental, spiritual, and physical unfoldment; or, in other words, his *right* to be rich.[58]

In New Thought philosophy, fulfillment is not possible without money. Everything exists in order to assist people in their pursuit of money. How does one attain the use of things? By the proper use of the mind and the exercise of faith. Thoughts will actualize desires in the physical realm.

In *Think and Grow Rich*, New Thought writer Napoleon Hill explains the acquisition of wealth this way:

> There comes, now, a statement which will give a better understanding of the importance of the principle of auto-suggestion assumed in the transmutation of desire into its physical, or monetary equivalent; namely: faith is a state of mind which may be induced, or created, by affirmation or repeated instructions to the subconscious mind, through the principle of auto-suggestion. . . . Repetition of affirmation of orders to your subconscious mind is the only known method of voluntary development of the emotion of faith.[59]

Moreover, Hill says that the main reason people do not achieve wealth is because "many people fail to impress Thinking Substance."[60] By the phrase "Thinking Substance," Hill refers to the divine. In other words, one has to form clear, mental images of what is desired, whether that is a house, a job, or some form of personal success. This positive thought, then, is the correct method to supernaturally achieve material wealth.

Robert Collier in *Secret of the Ages* further elaborates on the importance of clear, mental images, stating, "You can control those ideas through mind. Reduced to the ultimate—to the atom or to the electron—everything in this world is an idea of mind. All of it has been brought together through mind. If we can change the things we want back into mental images, we can multiply them as often as we like, possess all that we like."[61] Like Hill, Wattles, and Collier, Ernest Holmes contends that not only are thoughts critical to acquire success, but also spoken words are of great importance. Thoughts and words are forces that create reality. He writes, "If the word is the way that God creates, it is the right way. If it works for God, shall it not work for us? . . . All words have as much power as we put into them when we speak. 'The word is already in our own mouths.' That word is all that you will ever need to bring happiness, health and success to you."[62]

According to New Thought writers, then, in order to attain health and wealth, you must form a clear, distinct mental image of health and wealth and then take mental ownership of that picture. You must have faith that the object of your desire is already yours. As Wattles instructs, you simply "take possession of it [the mental picture], in mind, in the full faith that it is actually yours. Hold to this mental ownership; do not waiver for an instant in the faith that it is real."[63] If you want to be healthy and wealthy, then first realize that health and wealth is your right. Then you must think positive thoughts about your health and wealth. Within the New Thought system, the only reason you do not have the health and wealth you desire is because you think incorrectly. Since your thoughts and even your words create reality, simply visualize, believe, and speak the right words repeatedly and you will see your circumstances change.

Pillar Five: An Unorthodox View of Salvation

In light of the previous four pillars, it is, perhaps, not surprising to observe that New Thought writers advocate salvation by works. Given the self-centered trajectory of this philosophy, anything but a moralistic, works-based view of salvation would seem out of place.

Many New Thought writers, however, go beyond advocacy of salvation by works to outright denying the historic, orthodox doctrine of salvation by grace alone through faith. For example, in his commentary on the book of Revelation, Swedenborg rejects the atonement of Christ, writing, "It can now be seen that the Lord did not come into the world to propitiate the Father and to move Him to mercy, nor to bear our iniquities and thus take them away, nor that we might be saved by the imputation of His merit, or by intercession, or by immediate mercy, consequently not by a faith in these things, still less by the confidence of that faith."[64] Through his writings, Swedenborg claims that the key to divine bliss is the embrace of a moral life—with morality, of course, being defined by New Thought ideas.

Furthermore, according to New Thought, religion is not redemption from sin but simply the process of learning to love one's neighbor. Jesus was not the Son of God but merely a religious man whose spirit was raised from the dead. The International New Thought Alliance's Declaration of Principles does not mention sin, the exclusivity of Jesus for salvation, or the need for redemption. The clearest statement on the place of Christ is principle nine: "We affirm expression of the highest spiritual principle in loving one another unconditionally, promoting the highest good for all, teaching and healing one another, ministering to one another, and living together in peace, in accordance with the teachings of Jesus and other enlightened teachers."[65]

In addition to redefining salvation as ethical behavior, then, New Thought philosophy rejects the uniqueness of Jesus as the only way to salvation. Trine argues that all religions possess the truth and that we must find oneness with the Infinite.[66] The end result is that all religions are the same as they afford man the opportunity to discover the Infinite. According to New Thought, true religion will be attractive to all and repulsive to none. The gospel of New Thought is acceptable to everyone because it omits sin and each person defines the gospel for him- or herself.

In summary, for New Thought, salvation is not placing one's faith in Jesus Christ, the eternal Son of God, who died for the sins of humankind on the cross. Rather, salvation is a self-generated mystical experience with the Infinite, which entails channeling the divine influx for personal health, wealth, happiness, and success. New Thought advocate Nathan Wood articulates this teaching well in *The Secret of the Universe*. He contends that the people of Jesus' day "felt the influence of Jesus' marvelous personality. It entered other lives. It gave them new life. It made them over new, so much so that they were said to be born anew. It was vivid and real beyond all experience of personalities."[67]

CONCLUSION

While New Thought was adopted and espoused by some who claimed to be Christians, it is clear that New Thought ideas are not rooted in the Bible; rather, it shares commonalities with Hinduism, Oriental philosophy, the occult, and a general self-centered, pagan approach to life. New Thought distorts the biblical doctrine of God, emphasizes mind over matter, and exalts humans to the point that they can become godlike, if not divine. Moreover, New Thought teaches that the key to health and wealth is thinking, visualizing, and speaking the right words. Within this self-centered system, there is no place for Jesus' life, death, and resurrection.

While the differences between New Thought and Christian doctrine ought to be obvious, for many believers the lines are blurred. One reason for this is because New Thought ideas are often taught using biblical words and are justified by distorting Scripture. Many of the New Thought proponents were adept at taking pagan ideas and wrapping them in Scripture.

In the next chapter, we will survey the beginnings and the growth of the modern prosperity gospel movement using the five categorical pillars of New Thought. Rather than using quotations from New Thought writers to support the pillars, however, we will incorporate the words of modern prosperity preachers. The similarities between New Thought and the prosperity gospel are striking.

SUMMARY POINTS

- The prosperity gospel is built upon a quasi-Christian heresy, popular in the late nineteenth and early twentieth century, known as New Thought.
- Key New Thought thinkers include Emanuel Swedenborg, Phineas Quimby, Ralph Waldo Trine, and Norman Vincent Peale.

- New Thought is marked by a distorted view of God, an elevation of mind over matter, an exalted view of humankind, a focus upon attaining health and wealth, and an unorthodox view of salvation.
- New Thought teaches that the key to health and wealth acquisition is thinking, visualizing, and speaking the right words.
- New Thought ideas are often taught using biblical words and are justified by distorting Scripture.

Chapter 2

The Teachings of the Prosperity Gospel

I n the preceding chapter, we examined the foundations of the prosperity gospel—namely, the New Thought movement that flourished in the nineteenth and early twentieth century. In the present chapter, we will move our discussion to a study of the history and especially the teachings of the modern prosperity gospel. The teaching of this movement will be examined using the five categorical pillars of New Thought that were explored in chapter 1. What will become apparent is that the prosperity gospel is quite similar to the New Thought movement. By way of illustration, this chapter will conclude with an examination of the thought and teachings of Joel Osteen. We will show that Osteen, one of the most popular preachers in America, is an advocate of the prosperity gospel.

HISTORY OF THE PROSPERITY GOSPEL

As an organized movement, the prosperity gospel has only existed for about one hundred years, from the early nineteenth century up through the present time. While there have been dozens of prosperity gospel advocates during this time period, two stand out as preeminent: E. W. Kenyon and Kenneth E. Hagin. We will briefly review the ideas of Kenyon, who was one of the first to purposefully give New Thought an explicitly Christian veneer, and Hagin, who popularized the prosperity gospel through what became known as the Word of Faith movement.

E. W. Kenyon: Father of the Prosperity Gospel

In its modern form, the prosperity gospel can be traced to the thought of E. W. Kenyon (1867–1948), an evangelist, pastor, and founder of Bethel Bible Institute in Spencer, Massachusetts. Kenyon, born one year after the death of Phineas Quimby, the father of New Thought, synthesized New Thought philosophy with then contemporary theological trends.[1] Although Kenyon's writings reveal a level of critique against New Thought philosophy, they also demonstrate that, consciously or not, he incorporated New Thought teachings into his theological system. This is evidenced by Kenyon's advocacy of positive confession theology, his deficient view of the atonement, and his elevation of human beings, as well as his explicit teachings on health and wealth.[2]

In 1892 Kenyon attended the Emerson School of Oratory in Boston, a school where New Thought philosophy prevailed. Charles Emerson, the president of the school, was a minister of Unitarian and Universalist churches in New England and later became a practitioner of Christian Science. Influenced by Swedenborg's belief that the spiritual realm transcends the physical realm, Emerson taught a version of the gospel according to New Thought. Interestingly, Ralph Waldo Trine, the evangelist of New Thought, was a classmate of Kenyon at the Emerson School. While it is not clear exactly how much Kenyon observed while under Emerson's tutelage, as his later thought reveals, he clearly became familiar with the core tenets of New Thought. This is noteworthy since scholars recognize Kenyon to be the father of the modern prosperity gospel movement.

According to historian Dale Simmons, "Kenyon is the *primary* source of the health and wealth gospel of the independent Charismatic movement."[3] Kenyon's ideas influenced the prosperity gospel movement in several ways. First, his approach to theology is the basis for one of the prosperity gospel's most distinctive features—that is, speaking the right words to bring about a new reality.[4] Many even credit Kenyon with coining the popular prosperity gospel phrase, "What I confess, I possess."

Kenyon believed that positive confession is the key to prosperous living. Relating the power of confession to healing, Kenyon writes, "Confession always goes ahead of healing. Don't watch symptoms, watch the word, and be sure that your confession is bold and vigorous. Don't listen to people. Act on the word. Be a doer of the word. It is God speaking. You are healed. The word says you are. Don't listen to the senses. Give the word its place. God cannot lie."[5] According to Kenyon, then, with proper thoughts in one's spirit, one can command the physical world, including the physical body. He preached, "You will seldom rise above your words. If you talk sickness you will go to the level of your conversation. If you talk weakness and failure you will act it. You keep saying, 'I can't get work,' or 'I can't do this,' and your words react to your body. Why is this? It is because you are a spirit being. You are not a physical being. Basically you are a spirit and spirit registers words just as a piece of blotting paper takes ink."[6]

While Kenyon's positive confession teachings are troublesome, he has an even more serious theological error—that is, he believed that Jesus' death on the cross did not purchase salvation. Kenyon writes, "We have sung 'Nearer the Cross' and we have prayed that we might be 'Nearer the Cross' but the cross has no salvation in it. It is a place of failure and defeat."[7] Kenyon argues that the physical death of Jesus did not impact the sinful estate of humanity. He notes, "Sin basically is a spiritual thing, so it must be dealt with in the spirit realm. If Jesus paid the penalty of sin on the cross, then sin is but a physical act. If his death paid it, then every man could die for himself. Sin is in the spirit realm. This physical death was but a means to an end. . . . When Jesus died, his spirit was taken by the Adversary, and carried to the place where the sinner's spirit goes when he dies."[8] Kenyon believes that the real work of atonement was spiritual and not physical because he did not regard the humanity of Jesus as being important.

Like those in the New Thought movement, Kenyon places people at the center of his system. Religion's purpose is not to honor God or to redeem humanity but to serve people and help them get what they desire. Kenyon even teaches that people can make demands of God. He writes, "The value of an investment is its dividends. The value of Christianity is what we get out of it. We are Christians for what we can get in this life, and we claim a hope of a world to come, where pain and sorrow cannot claim us as victims, and death cannot cut short our joys. We also demand that the God we serve and worship shall hear our petitions, protect us in danger, comfort us in sorrow."[9] Clearly, in Kenyon's system, a relationship with God is a means for a person to get what he or she wants. As with New Thought, then, the purpose of the divine being is to ensure one's own well-being and success.

When we go into partnership with [God], and we learn His ways of doing business, we cannot be failures.

E. W. Kenyon

Healing and prosperity belong to Kenyon's teachings as well. If one partners with God, he teaches, life will be good because God does not want people to experience hardship or failure. Given this guarantee of success, Kenyon asserts that it is mere common sense to be in relationship with God. Kenyon writes:

> God never planned that we should live in poverty, physical, mental or spiritual. He made Israel go to the head of the nations financially. When we go into partnership with Him, and we learn His ways of doing business, we cannot be failures. Failures are not God-made. God never made a weakling or an inefficient man. He is purely a human product. . . . You can't be a failure, for His wisdom is your wisdom; His ability in every department of life is your ability. All you need to do is to study the Word of God and get the knowledge that is imparted to you there. Then He will give you the ability to make your life a success.[10]

Though it is debatable whether Kenyon intentionally incorporated New Thought philosophy into his religious system, at a minimum he is guilty of blending New Thought with Christianity and thereby creating a false gospel. John Kennington, who knew Kenyon personally, noticed the similarities between New Thought and Kenyon's teaching. Kennington claimed that Kenyon even admitted to him that he drew from the well of New Thought.[11]

Certainly New Thought writers use the Bible, talk about Jesus, and speak with religious jargon, but they also use their own definitions and shape the Christian message for their own purposes. This is what makes New Thought so dangerous—that is, it is false doctrine disguised in biblical language. Unfortunately, New Thought influenced Kenyon and thereby provided the foundation for the prosperity gospel. Later Kenneth E. Hagin embraced and spread Kenyon's core teachings with success.

Kenneth E. Hagin: Evangelist of the Prosperity Gospel

In the late 1940s, Oral Roberts burst onto the religious scene with his ministry of alleged healing and financial prosperity. While Roberts certainly captured national attention and spread prosperity theology, the late Kenneth E. Hagin (1917–2003) is recognized by most to be the greatest evangelist of the prosperity gospel, as well as being the father of the Word of Faith movement. This movement subscribes to practical charismatic beliefs (e.g., speaking in tongues, baptism of the Holy Spirit, miraculous gifts) and emphasizes the prosperity gospel. More than any other organization, the Word of Faith movement is the vehicle that was responsible for spreading prosperity teachings across the United States in the late twentieth century.

Hagin was born in Texas in 1917, and his call to ministry occurred when he was a teenager. According to his official biography, "In April 1933 during a dramatic conversion experience, Hagin reported dying three times in 10 minutes, each time seeing the horrors of hell and then returning to life. In August 1934, Rev. Hagin was miraculously healed, raised off a deathbed by the power of God and the revelation of faith in God's Word. Jesus appeared to Rev. Hagin eight times over the next several years in visions that changed the course of his ministry."[12] Note that a common feature of prosperity teachers is their reliance upon extrabiblical revelation from God. Many leaders in this movement claim to receive special messages from God and this, in turn, gives them greater authority in the eyes of their followers.

In 1962, Hagin established his own evangelistic ministry for the purpose of propagating his doctrines. As a part of this ministry, Hagin had a syndicated radio program, founded Rhema Bible Training Center in Tulsa, Oklahoma, started *Word of Faith* magazine, produced numerous books, and had an evangelistic television ministry. An Assemblies of God preacher, Hagin claimed to be an anointed prophet and teacher of faith. In several works, he claims to have had numerous personal visitations with Jesus who provided him new revelation that was to be taught to the church.[13] In *How to Write Your Own Ticket with God*, Hagin recounts Jesus' personal appearance to him in which Jesus dictates the message, "Say it. Do it. Receive it. Tell it."[14]

In 1988, scholar D. R. McConnell, a critic of the prosperity gospel, linked Hagin's teachings, in part, directly to Kenyon. In his work, entitled *A Different Gospel*, McConnell provides verbatim quotations from several of Hagin's sermons, demonstrating that Hagin plagiarized Kenyon's work.[15] McConnell shows how Hagin mixed Kenyon's teachings with Scripture, thus making his material palatable to the church and impervious to criticism since he sounded like a biblical scholar and a mystical seer who had divine encounters with Jesus.[16] Yet, Hagin was not alone in promoting the prosperity teachings. Numerous other preachers adopted Hagin's New Thought tainted doctrine and started their own ministries. Collectively, these ministries formed what is known as the Word of Faith movement. Examples include Hagin's son, Kenneth Hagin Jr., Kenneth Copeland, Frederick Price, Robert Tilton, Benny Hinn, Charles Capps, Jerry Savelle, and many others.

While there is not a Word of Faith or prosperity gospel denomination, there are many organizations that assist the ministries of prosperity advocates.[17] For example, in 1973 Paul and Jan Crouch, along with Jim and Tammy Faye Bakker, founded the Trinity Broadcast Network. According to its Web site, TBN is now the world's largest Christian television network. TBN serves as a platform for prosperity theology teachers to reach larger audiences. Examples of such teachers include Rod Parsley, Creflo Dollar, Paula White, Kenneth Copeland, Jesse Duplantis, and Kenneth Hagin Jr. In the 1980s, the Jimmy Swaggart and Jim Bakker financial and sex scandals shook the Word of Faith movement; yet, it has since recovered and flourishes again today.

While modern prosperity preachers would likely deny that their message is rooted in the pagan philosophy and secular thinking of the New Thought movement, a study of their teachings suggests otherwise. If Kenyon incorporated New Thought ideas into his religious teachings, and if Hagin was influenced by Kenyon, it stands to reason that the prosperity teachers who have followed Hagin may reflect New Thought ideas. Using the five categorical pillars of New Thought from the previous chapter, we will investigate the teachings of the prosperity gospel to see if there is any overlap with New Thought beliefs.

THE TEACHINGS OF PROSPERITY THEOLOGY

The prosperity gospel is quite popular in the United States, and it is being exported to other parts of the world, especially South America and Africa. Prosperity preachers, including soft advocates of the prosperity gospel such as Joel Osteen, T. D. Jakes, and Joyce Meyer, are well-known names and each has a significant following. Without question, many prosperity teachers are sincere, passionate, and excellent communicators, but these qualities do not excuse false teachings, whether intentional or not. Many genuine Christians listen to prosperity teachers but do not discern how prosperity teachers distort Scripture and the gospel. Of course, taken at face value, the prosperity message—God wants you to be prosperous in everything in the here-and-now—sounds good, but is not found in Scripture.

Most Christians fail to realize that in addition to misunderstanding the true nature of the gospel, many who preach the prosperity message hold to heretical views of God, Christ, and people, among other errors. Given their emphasis on material prosperity, their views on such doctrines are not prominent in their popular writings, but are nevertheless present, and have been well-documented.[18] One danger in attempting to outline the theology of the prosperity gospel is that the movement is quite broad, and every prosperity teacher has his or her own unique theological nuances. This caution notwithstanding, there is still a significant pattern of doctrinal deviation among prosperity teachers. In the following five categorical pillars, we will see that the ideas of the New Thought movement, as well as other theological errors, form the foundation for much of the modern prosperity movement.

Pillar One: A Distorted View of God

Many believers in the prosperity gospel do not realize that several prominent prosperity gospel teachers deny the biblical doctrine of the Trinity. These teachers reject the orthodox view that God is one in essence and yet also three in person, coequal and coeternal. Instead, many advocates of the prosperity gospel believe that God is one in person and that He appears at various times in different modes as the Father, the Son, or the Holy Spirit. In other words, God is not simultaneously the Father, Son, and the Holy Spirit. This view of the Trinity is the ancient heresy known as modalism.

An example of a soft advocate of the prosperity gospel with such a belief is T. D. Jakes, who has been called "America's Preacher." Jakes is a member of the Oneness Pentecostal movement, a group known for its unorthodox view of the Trinity. The church over which Jakes presides, the Potter's House in Dallas, Texas, believes that "there is one God, Creator of all things, infinitely perfect, and eternally existing in three manifestations: Father, Son and Holy Spirit."[19] While this statement sounds orthodox, it is nevertheless problematic.[20] The term "manifestations" is typical of Oneness Pentecostal theology. Jakes has issued statements attempting to clarify his view of the Trinity, but Pastor Lawrence Robinson, a close friend and a staff member at the Potter's House, has affirmed that Jakes denies the historically orthodox doctrine of the Trinity.[21]

In 1990, Benny Hinn made blasphemous claims under the guise of new revelation from the Holy Spirit. He claimed that each person of the Godhead is triune, resulting in nine total persons.[22] Hinn later tried to clarify his statement, yet his current belief about God is unclear as it sounds similar to Jakes's view on the Trinity. Hinn's doctrinal statement reads, "The one true God has revealed Himself as the eternally self-existent, self-revealed 'I AM' and has further revealed Himself as embodying the principles of relationship and association, i.e., Father, Son, and Holy Ghost (Deuteronomy 6:4; Mark 12:29; Isaiah 43:10, 11; Matthew 28:19)."[23] It is not clear what "embodying the principles of relationship and association" means.

Creflo Dollar, pastor of World Changers Church International in Georgia, also denies the historically orthodox doctrine of the Trinity. His view of the Trinity appears to be similar to that of Jakes and Hinn. In a World Changers program on February 19, 2001, Dollar claimed that there is one God who has three different functions. He explains his view with the illustration of himself, being one person, yet at the same time, a husband, a father, and a pastor. While his illustration has the veneer of orthodoxy, it does not accurately describe the Trinity because God is one in essence and simultaneously three in person. Conversely, Dollar is one person with three different roles or responsibilities. He is not three persons. Dollar's view of the Trinity, then, like Jakes and Hinn, appears to be essentially equivalent to modalism. With the exception of affirming that Jesus is the Son of God, the World Changers statement of belief takes no specific position on the Trinity, and hardly even mentions God.[24]

Kenneth Copeland, another popular prosperity teacher with his own ministry, also keeps his doctrinal statement about the Trinity quite brief: "We believe in one God—Father, Son and Holy Spirit, Creator of all things." As with other prosperity preachers, the problem is not what Copeland's doctrinal statement says; rather, the problem is its brevity and what it does not say. This is especially problematic in light of Copeland's association with known modalists, such as T. D. Jakes.

The prosperity teachers not only confuse the doctrine of the Trinity, but they also make outrageous—or, at least, irresponsible—statements about God. For example, Copeland asserts that God is a failure, saying, "I was shocked when I found out who the biggest failure in the Bible actually is. . . . The biggest one in the whole Bible is God. . . . Now, the reason you don't think of God as a failure is He never said He's a failure. And you're not a failure till you say you're one."[25] As will be demonstrated as the following pillars are reviewed, prosperity teachers also demote God, stripping Him of His sovereignty, and place humans at the center of their theological system.

**I was shocked when I found out
who the biggest failure in the Bible actually is....
The biggest one in the whole Bible is God.**
Kenneth Copeland

Pillar Two: An Elevation of Mind over Matter

Much like the proponents of New Thought, many prosperity preachers believe that words—both thought and spoken—are a force and have creative power. In his book *The Tongue, A Creative Force*, Pastor Charles Capps summarizes the prosperity doctrine of mind over matter as he writes, "The creative ability of man comes through his spirit. He speaks spirit words that work in the world of the spirit. They will also dominate the physical world. He breathes spirit life into God's Word and it becomes a living substance, working for him as it worked for God in the beginning. These spirit words dominate the natural world."[26]

Creflo Dollar further explains the relationship between the spiritual and physical world. In a message dated June 2, 2009, he preached, "The spiritual world is the parent of the physical world. Everything came from God, who is a spirit. The physical matter, including circumstances and situations, is physical substance. We can use spiritual substance to change physical substance. Spiritual laws supersede physical laws. Jesus superseded the law of gravity when He walked on water.... As believers, we have authority over this physical world."[27] Dollar, then, believes that the immaterial supersedes the material. Therefore, by tapping into the right spiritual laws, one can control physical matter, circumstances, and situations.

According to the prosperity gospel, speaking the right words combined with faith in those words can produce amazing results because

God established spiritual laws that govern this world. The believer's task is to use words in order to exercise spiritual laws for their own benefit. If believers repeat the right words and believe, then God must bless, for spiritual laws are in effect. Conversely, a lack of positive thinking, coupled with a lack of faith, will hinder God from working on behalf of people. To change one's circumstances or to get God to work things out, believers must be proactive with their confessions.

Not surprisingly, positive confession is foundational to the prosperity gospel. It refers to speaking the right words in order to create the future. Speaking again of the power of positive confession, Creflo Dollar says, "God uses words to create what he wants to exist. Christians have the same ability. For example, when there is lack in your life, call forth abundance to replace it. Say what you believe is true according to the Word. This is not denying what exists. We speak the desired result. When you need healing, say what the Bible says, 'By his stripes I am healed.'"[28]

**God uses words to create what he wants to exist.
Christians have the same ability.
For example, when there is lack in your life,
call forth abundance to replace it.
Say what you believe is true according to the Word.**
Creflo Dollar

The prosperity teachers' theological rationale is simple, but false. They start with the valid premise that God created the world by speaking—that is, He used words (see Gen. 1:3). Since humans are made in the image of God (see Gen. 1:26–27), prosperity advocates conclude that they too can use words in order to create new situations. If God's words have creative, miraculous power, then human words ought to have the same characteristics. Yet, here is a problem: although God did speak the world into existence, and God did make humanity in His own image, it does not follow that people have the same power as God. In order to make the prosperity doctrine of mind over matter function, you have to assume that being made in the image of God means having the same power as God. This assumption, however, is false for it fails to recognize the distinction between an infinite being (God) and finite beings (humans). To be consistent in prosperity gospel thinking, if people do have the same power to create as God, then they should be able to create new objects out of nothing.

Kenneth Copeland also believes in the power of words. He claims that believers can have whatever they speak because God has created the whole world for human benefit.[29] In his article "Applying Faith in Prayer," Copeland guarantees, "Once you have prayed in faith, hold fast to your confession. God is aware of your situation. His power went to work the instant you prayed in faith. You can now rest assured that what you prayed will come to pass. Maintain your faith by keeping your confession."[30] Copeland explains further the power of words and the laws, stating, "Speak only words that agree with what you desire. Jesus is seated at the right hand of the Father. As your High Priest, He is seeing to it that the whole system works the way God said it would! The importance of speaking right words cannot be measured. Faith is released with the mouth. Words are the vehicles. God spoke faith-filled words when He created the universe. . . . God spoke and the Spirit of God used the faith in those words to create the worlds."[31] Again, the idea is that if God can create out of nothing, then people can too. Notice, however, that Copeland thinks that it was God's faith in His words that created the world. In Copeland's twisted theology, even the God of the universe needs faith.

Since positive confession is the key to guaranteeing blessing, some prosperity teachers provide lists of confessions for their followers. Joyce Meyer is one such teacher. She compiled a list of confessions to be repeated each day. While some of the statements are biblical, others are not. Like other prosperity teachers, she claims that if one repeats these confessions, then they will materialize. Her list contains what she desires to be true in her life. Like Copeland, her statements are guarantees. Here is a sample:

- I prosper in everything I put my hand to. I have prosperity in all areas of my life—spiritually, financially, mentally, and socially.
- I take good care of my body. I eat right, I look good, I feel good, and I weigh what God wants me to weigh.
- Pain cannot successfully come against my body because Jesus bore all my pain.
- I lay hands on the sick, and they recover.
- I receive speaking engagements in person, by phone, and/or by mail every day.
- I walk in the spirit all of the time.[32]

These positive confessions are simply positive thinking. They work just like New Thought's law of attraction: you attract what you think about. As with New Thought, visualizing success and speaking it into existence activate the spiritual laws in the world.

According to Joel Osteen, whose ministry will be considered in greater detail at the end of this chapter, you have to see your success in your mind because what you see in your mind is what you produce. If you see yourself in a new situation, then God can bring it to pass. Along with visualization, Osteen uses words to be successful. He has his own version of the law of attraction. He suggests, "Our thoughts contain tremendous power. Remember, we draw into our lives that which we constantly think about. If we're always dwelling on the negative, we will attract negative people, experiences, and attitudes."[33] He continues, "Our words have tremendous power, and whether we want to or not, we will give life to what we're saying, either good or bad. . . . Words are similar to seeds, by speaking them aloud, they are planted in our subconscious minds, and they take on a life of their own."[34]

For the prosperity gospel, then, words are a force and possess the power to create—mind over matter. Until believers visualize, speak, and believe in their words, God cannot act on their behalf. The spiritual laws that God established must be obeyed. Sadly, though, with such teachings the prosperity teachers denigrate God and turn Him into a genie in a bottle who exists to serve people once the right words are spoken.

Pillar Three: An Exalted View of Humankind

Prosperity theology inverts the relationship between the Creator and the creature. Human beings are now at the center of the universe; therefore, God simply exists in order to meet all of their needs, including good relationships, sound health, and financial gains. This gospel is human-centered and, thus, egotistical. Prosperity gospel preachers remind their flocks that they have God's favor upon all aspects of their lives. For example, Joel Osteen, in reference to being aware of God's favor, says, "Consequently—and I say this humbly—I've come to expect to be treated differently. I've learned to expect people to want to help me. My attitude is this: I'm a child of the Most High God. My Father created the whole universe. He has crowned me with favor; therefore, I can expect preferential treatment. I can expect people to go out of their way to want to help me."[35] Note carefully what Osteen is saying. Not only does God exist to serve people, but everyone else exists to serve me. Does Osteen's statement reflect Jesus' teaching when He taught His disciples to be humble, saying, "For even the Son of Man came not to be served but to serve, and to give his life as a ransom for many" (Mark 10:45)? The biblical call to sacrifice, humility, and suffering is notably absent in prosperity theology.

The overemphasis on people within this movement is not surprising since many prosperity advocates view human beings to be divine. Paul Crouch infamously remarked, "I am a little god. Critics, be gone!"[36] Kenneth Copeland concurred, "You don't have a God in you, you are one."[37] These ridiculous claims illustrate one of the reasons why a self-centered gospel is so attractive. While the Bible does teach that human beings are made in the image of God (see Gen. 1:27) and that they partake of the divine nature (see 2 Peter 1:4), it never teaches that people are divine. There is only one God and the Scriptures declare, "'You are my witnesses,' declares the LORD, 'and my servant whom I have chosen, that you may know and believe me and understand that I am he. Before me no god was formed, nor shall there be any after me. I, I am the LORD, and besides me there is no savior'" (Isa. 43:10–11).

A typical verse used by proponents of the prosperity gospel to support the deification of human beings is Psalm 82:6, which states, "I said,

'You are gods, sons of the Most High, all of you.'" Interestingly, however, the following verse is often overlooked. Psalm 82:7 reads, "Nevertheless, like men you shall die, and fall like any prince." Taking the verse in the entire context of Psalm 82 enables the reader to see that verse 6 refers to corrupt judges who presume to be gods in their positions, and God reminds them that they are mortal.[38] Like Crouch and Copeland before him, Creflo Dollar, in a sermon on Psalm 82 delivered January 21, 2001, entitled "Our Equality with God Through Righteousness," alleges that man is a god.[39]

T. D. Jakes makes a more subtle claim that people are divine. He teaches that human beings possess the DNA of God—thus, they were made out of God. Jakes preaches, "When God created Adam, He created him from the dust of the earth. God put His mouth on him; blew in him the breath of life. He became a living soul. God said, 'I wanted to see what I looked like so I made you to be in My image. You have My DNA. You [are] created out of Me. You're a derivative of Me.'"[40]

There are a number of problems with Jakes's message. First, the Bible does not teach that people are made out of God. Instead, it teaches that they were made by God. Jakes's version of creation, like New Thought, appears to be a form of panentheism—that is, the idea that humans are literally a part of God. Second, the Bible does not teach that God needed to make people to be able to see Himself. God the Father is a spirit and, as such, does not have a physical body (see John 4:24). Instead, the Bible teaches that God created humanity for His own purposes and glory (see Isa. 43:7). Third, the Bible does not teach that the image of God means that people have "God genes," so to speak. When Jakes equates DNA with the image of God, it is both confusing and dangerous. Unfortunately, this type of teaching, which is irresponsible preaching at best and heresy at worst, is far too common among prosperity teachers.

Pillar Four: A Focus on Health and Wealth

While advocates of the prosperity gospel preach and teach on a wide variety of subjects, the core of their message is material prosperity. Several prosperity teachers are on record as teaching that neither Jesus nor

His disciples were poor. The title of Oral Roberts's book *How I Learned Jesus Was Not Poor* captures this idea well. Creflo Dollar thinks that since the soldiers at the foot of the cross were gambling over what he believes to be Jesus' expensive robe, Jesus must have been quite wealthy. He claims, "When you go to the Scriptures, there is no way you can conclude Jesus was poor."[41] T. D. Jakes, whose personal fortune is estimated at one hundred million dollars, has suggested that Jesus was rich since He had to support the apostles.[42] Moreover, the classic example of poverty being eschewed is Robert Tilton who believes that being poor is a sin because God promises prosperity.[43]

One of the most striking characteristics of prosperity teachers is their seeming fixation with the act of giving. Students of the prosperity gospel are urged to give generously and are confronted with such pious statements as, "True prosperity is the ability to use God's power to meet the needs of mankind in any realm of life,"[44] and, "We have been called to finance the gospel to the world."[45] While at face value these statements appear to be praiseworthy, a closer examination of the theology behind them reveals that the prosperity gospel's emphasis on giving is built on anything but philanthropic motives. The driving force behind this emphasis on giving is what teacher Robert Tilton referred to as the "Law of Compensation."[46] According to this law, which prosperity teachers derive from passages such as Ecclesiastes 11:1, Mark 10:30, 2 Corinthians 9:6, and Galatians 6:7, Christians need to give generously because when they do, God gives back more in return. This, in turn, leads to a cycle of ever-increasing prosperity.

As Gloria Copeland puts it, "Give $10 and receive $1,000; give $1,000 and receive $100,000. . . . In short, Mark 10:30 is a very good deal."[47] It is clear that the prosperity gospel's doctrine of giving is built upon faulty motives. Whereas Jesus teaches His disciples, "Lend, expecting nothing in return" (Luke 6:35), prosperity theologians teach their disciples to lend because they will get a great return. One cannot help but agree with author Edward Pousson's observation that "the prosperity message is in captivity to the American dream."[48]

Moreover, prosperity teachers make promises to their followers that are simply not true. They teach that it is God's will for them to be financially successful and healthy. Kenneth Copeland stated, "You must realize that it is God's will for you to prosper. This is available to you, and frankly, it would be stupid of you not to partake of it."[49] Paula White agrees, "Do you believe that God wants you to live in the abundance and the overflow of His goodness, His mercy, and His provision? King David declared that God takes pleasure in you prospering. God is not magnified when you are broke, busted, or disgusted."[50] In their view of God, then, the Lord is most glorified when you are satisfied in your wealth. Until all God's people are wealthy and healthy, the Lord does not receive the glory due His name. The idea that we should honor God despite our circumstances is absent from the prosperity gospel.

God is not magnified when you are broke, busted, or disgusted.
Paula White

To their credit, prosperity preachers are careful to point out that prosperity means much more than money, but their words often suggest that money is the primary focus. For example, Creflo Dollar says, "The Word of God is your highway to the world of wealth (Job 22:21–22). If you take the seed of God's Word and put it in your heart, then wealth and riches will be in your house (Psalm 112:1–3). Seek out people who are sent with the message of prosperity to break the poverty chain."[51] In other words, follow prosperity teachers. They know where the money is.

At a gathering of the prosperity gospel faithful in August 2009, reflecting upon a downturn in the economy, Gloria Copeland preached, "God knows where the money is, and he knows how to get the money to you."[52] Preacher Jerry Savelle added, "Any time a worried thought about money pops up in your mind the next thing you do is sow. Stop worrying, start sowing. That's God's stimulus package for you."[53] The message, then, is clear: give to the ministry, plant a financial seed, and God will give you a return on that act of faith.

For the most successful prosperity teachers, this formula works and their followers see their success. Numerous prosperity teachers are millionaires and have extravagant tastes. Take, for instance, Joyce Meyer. She boldly asserts that God made her rich. Meyer tells her audience, "If you stay in your faith, you are going to get paid. I am now living in my reward."[54] Her ministry takes in roughly ninety-five million dollars per year, and her headquarters display her wealth. Although Meyer's ministry is only one example, it is undeniable that the prosperity gospel is big business. The amount of wealth being channeled into prosperity ministries has caught the attention of the U.S. Senate Finance Committee. With famous preachers flaunting their wealth, it is not surprising that the Senate Finance Committee is investigating six ministries, all of which promote prosperity theology, to ensure there has not been misuse of donations.[55]

**If you stay in your faith, you are going to get paid.
I am now living in my reward.**
Joyce Meyer

Although advocates of the prosperity gospel primarily focus on being financially successful, promises of healing and good health are part of their message too. Listen to Hagin's claim: "I believe that it is the plan of God our Father that no believer should ever be sick. . . . It is not—I state boldly—it is not the will of God my Father that we should suffer with cancer and other dread diseases which bring pain and anguish. No! It is God's will that we be healed."[56] While Hagin's claim may be true from an eternal perspective, he fails to incorporate the temporal effects of the fall of humankind into his theology.

Some prosperity teachers clearly recognize the need for medical assistance, but still encourage their followers to take the higher road of faith. In Fred Price's ministry magazine, Robert Bolden discusses asthma and its causes and treatments. After describing the medications for asthma and encouraging people to consult a doctor for treatment, Bolden tells the reader to claim their right to be healed. He advises:

> As a believer we understand that healing belongs to us as a covenant right. We also must exercise our rights by using God's Word concerning healing. Isaiah 53:4–5, Matthew 8:17, 1 Peter 2:24, clearly these scriptures tell us that healing belongs to us. We see also in Philippians 2:9, "Therefore God also has highly exalted Him and given Him the name which is above every name." So, we have the right and privilege to use that name against asthma and everything that is associated with it. In Mark 11:23 the Word says that whosoever says to this mountain, be removed and be cast into the sea, and does not doubt in his heart, but believes that those things he says will be done, he will have whatever he says. In this case the mountain is asthma, and we say to asthma be removed and be cast into the sea, and not doubt![57]

Bolden captures the prosperity teaching on healing; it is your right to be healed and you only need to exercise faith.

To be healed, Joyce Meyer teaches that believers should dwell on God's Word, which brings healing to the flesh. She writes, "The key to partaking of the life and healing energy in the Word is feeding on it until it penetrates your spirit where it deposits that life and energy."[58] This sounds quite similar to New Thought philosophy as apparently Meyer believes that people can initiate and direct spiritual power over the material world. Additionally, in her writings Meyer prescribes numerous healing confessions, many of which make assertions that are simply not true. Here is one example:

> "I will" is the strongest assertion that can be made in the English language. God is speaking to me now saying, "I will take sickness away from the midst of thee." God is watching over this Word, performing it in me now. He is taking sickness away from the midst of me. Good-bye, sickness! The Lord is taking you away from the

midst of me. Thank You, Father, for taking sickness away from me. I thank You for doing what You said. . . . I'm abiding under the shadow of Jehovah-Rapha, the Lord that healeth me. No plague shall come nigh my dwelling or my body. I resist sickness and disease. I refuse to accept it! It's not mine! I refuse to be sick in Jesus' Name. Sickness cannot trespass in my body. Sickness, *(name it)*, you can't come nigh my dwelling. I refuse you! I resist you![59]

Prosperity teachers are adamant about the right of people to be healed because they believe that God provided physical healing in the death of His Son, Jesus. Among others, their proof-texts for this teaching include Isaiah 53:5, "and with his stripes we are healed," and 1 Peter 2:24, "He himself bore our sins in his body on the tree. . . . By his wounds you have been healed." As the next chapter will show, though, the primary meaning of verses such as Isaiah 53:5 and 1 Peter 2:24 is that believers are healed of their sin by what Christ accomplished on the cross. But this is not the only error that prosperity advocates make in regard to the cross; they also misunderstand the purpose of the cross.

Pillar Five: An Unorthodox View of Salvation

Taken at face value, many prosperity preachers appear to have orthodox views of salvation. Many of those within the prosperity movement openly invite listeners to trust in Jesus for salvation. For example, after stating that Jesus is the Son of God and that He died, was buried, and rose again, Creflo Dollar says, "Where you spend eternity is based on your decision to make Jesus Christ your Lord and Savior."[60] Joyce Meyer makes a clear statement about salvation as well. In her ministry's belief statement, she writes, "We can have a personal relationship with God through salvation, God's free gift to man. It is not a result of what we do, but it is only available through God's unearned favor."[61] Joel Osteen, at the end of each broadcast, invites people to place faith in Jesus.

In spite of these seemingly orthodox statements about salvation, however, several significant problems arise. First, some prosperity preachers have a skewed view of the Christ in whom they encourage their followers to trust. For instance, Kenneth Copeland teaches that Jesus completely emptied Himself of His divinity while on earth. Copeland remarked, "Why didn't Jesus openly proclaim himself as God during his 33 years on earth? For one single reason. He hadn't come to earth as God, he'd come as man."[62] To clarify, while Copeland apparently believes that Jesus is or became God, he also believes that Jesus ceased to be God during His incarnation. Copeland challenges the doubter to "search the Gospels for yourself. If you do, you'll find what I say is true."[63] Likewise, Creflo Dollar echoes Copeland's beliefs about Jesus. In a December 8, 2002 message tellingly entitled *Jesus' Growth into Sonship*, he preached:

> But Jesus didn't show up perfect, he grew into his perfection. You know Jesus, in one Scripture in the Bible he went on a journey, and he was tired. You better hope God don't get tired. Isaiah 50 says, 50, 60, somewhere, says where we have a God who fainteth not, neither is weary. But Jesus did, if he came as God and he got tired, he says he sat down by the well because he was tired. Boy we're in trouble. And somebody said, well, Jesus came as God. Well, how many of you know the Bible says God never sleeps nor slumbers? And yet in the book of Mark we see Jesus asleep in the back of the boat. Now please listen to me, please listen to me. This ain't no heresy. I am not some false prophet, I am just reading this thing out to you from the Bible.[64]

The problem, illustrated by the teachings of Copeland and Dollar, is this: belief in a false Christ is misplaced trust and is insufficient for salvation. Only Jesus, the God-Man, can save people from sin.

Second, prosperity teachers misunderstand Jesus' death on the cross for the sin of the world. For example, Kenneth Hagin limits Christ's atonement to His spiritual death, not His physical death. Hagin claims, "Jesus tasted spiritual death for every man. And his Spirit and inner man went to hell in my place. Can't you see that? Physical death wouldn't remove your sins. He's tasted death for every man. He's talking about tasting spiritual death."[65] Hagin is not the only preacher who rejects Jesus' physical death as payment for sin. Frederick K. C. Price makes the same error. He preached, "Do you think the punishment for our sin was to die on a cross? . . . No, the punishment was to go into hell itself."[66] These representative statements illustrate the prosperity gospel's distortion of the orthodox, biblical doctrine of the atonement. Scripture teaches that Jesus made possible reconciliation with God through His physical death on the cross (see 2 Cor. 5:21). While Jesus' descent into hell is surely a debated topic,[67] what is clear is the fact that Christ made atonement for sin upon the cross, not in the bowels of hell.

Third, although some prosperity preachers appear to articulate an orthodox doctrine of salvation, an important question is, "From what does Jesus save people?" Of course, the biblical answer is sin; yet, from listening to some advocates of the prosperity gospel, one might conclude that Jesus saves people from a nonprosperous life. The point is this: while many prosperity teachers offer the plan of salvation, they undermine the gospel with their teaching. The focus of the prosperity gospel is not God but humans. The prosperity gospel is little more than a self-help program designed to aid people in their pursuit of material success. Despite saying the right words about salvation, the prosperity teachers offer a false gospel that does not save anyone. Gordon Fee, a prolific New Testament scholar, observes, "American Christianity is rapidly being infected by an insidious disease, the so-called 'wealth and health' Gospel—although it has very little of the character of the Gospel in it."[68]

SUMMARY

After looking at the teachings of the prosperity gospel through the lens of the five categorical pillars of New Thought, it is clear that there are similarities between these two movements. Both New Thought and the prosperity gospel exhibit a distorted view of God, an elevation of mind over matter, an exalted view of people, a focus on health and wealth, and an unorthodox view of salvation. While prosperity preachers would likely not acknowledge their dependence upon New Thought, whether consciously aware of it or not, it is nonetheless present.

EXCURSUS: THE TEACHINGS OF JOEL OSTEEN

We realize that not every prosperity teacher adheres to all of the ideas mentioned in this chapter. The prosperity gospel is such a large and diverse movement that, apart from a common emphasis on material flourishing, it is impossible to comprehensively summarize the beliefs of all prosperity teachers. With this in mind, however, we wanted to call the reader's attention to one of the more common manifestations of the prosperity gospel in modern culture—that is, the teachings of the so-called soft advocates of the prosperity gospel. Soft advocates of the prosperity gospel can be distinguished from their more radical counterparts, such as Hagin and Copeland, in that soft advocates tend to mix more orthodox theology into their messages. The most well-known soft advocate of the prosperity gospel in twenty-first century America is Joel Osteen.

Joel Osteen is the pastor of Lakewood Church in Houston, Texas, the largest church in America, with a weekly attendance of approximately forty thousand. Osteen assumed the leadership of Lakewood Church after the death of his father, John Osteen, and continues to experience tremendous growth in the church and notoriety in the media. In 2004, Joel Osteen released *Your Best Life Now: 7 Steps to Living at Your Full Potential,* and the book quickly ascended to the top of the *New York Times* best-seller list and has since sold approximately four million copies. His 2007 sequel, *Become a Better You: 7 Keys to Improving Your Life Every Day,* sold equally well. Osteen's latest volume, *It's Your Time: Activate Your Faith, Achieve Your Dreams, and Increase in God's Favor,* published in late 2009, is currently near the top of the *New York Times* best-seller list.

Since Osteen became the senior pastor of Lakewood in 1999, the church has grown from approximately eight thousand to forty thousand. Lakewood's services are televised on numerous television networks that reach roughly two hundred million households per week and can be seen in one hundred countries worldwide. In 2005, Lakewood moved into the former Compaq Center in Houston, and with a ninety-million-dollar renovation, the arena was transformed into a sixteen-thousand-seat auditorium.

In short, Osteen is the most visible and popular preacher in America and is considered to be a leader of evangelicals. He has appeared on numerous national programs such as *60 Minutes, Larry King Live,* and on the Fox News channel. While Osteen certainly appears genuine and sincere in his faith, his prosperity message is anything but harmless. In what follows, it will be shown that, among other errors, Osteen misinterprets Scripture, misunderstands the gospel, and lacks theological conviction.

The Scriptures

Paul writes to Timothy, "Do your best to present yourself to God as one approved, a worker who has no need to be ashamed, rightly handling the word of truth" (2 Tim. 2:15). A preacher must be competent to interpret Scripture with accuracy and integrity. Yet, on several occasions Osteen has demonstrated a lack of competence. For example, in *Your Best Life Now,* Osteen references the story of the lame man at the pool of Bethesda in John 5.[69] Osteen's retelling and interpretation of this passage are questionable. First, Osteen makes a factual error. He reverses the order of the events in the text. After paraphrasing Jesus' response to the man, Osteen completes the story with his own conclusion, writing, "When the man did what Jesus told him to do, he was miraculously healed."[70] The text actually says, "Jesus said to him, 'Get up, take up your bed, and walk.' And at once the man was healed, and he took up his bed and walked. Now that day was the Sabbath" (John 5:8–9). Note that it was when Jesus spoke that the man was instantly healed and then he stood up and walked. Perhaps Osteen accidentally reversed the order of events, but his interpretation reflects his theology—just obey and God will bless or heal you. Moreover, Osteen's mistake actually detracts from the central person in the narrative, Jesus Christ.

Second, Osteen allegorizes the meaning of the text and, therefore, proposes an illegitimate application of the passage. According to Osteen, the point of the story is, "If you're serious about being well, if you really want to be made physically and emotionally whole, you must get up and get moving with your life."[71] Is this the reason John recorded this event in the life of Jesus? In the larger context of the gospel of John, which

Osteen seems to have overlooked, John recorded the healing of the lame man in order to display the power of Jesus, to demonstrate that Jesus was the Son of God, and to lead into the later discussion about the Sabbath and the divinity of Christ.[72]

If this were the only example of questionable exegesis, one might concede that every pastor has engaged in an occasional interpretational blunder, but Osteen habitually justifies his message with suspicious interpretations of Scripture. In *Become a Better You*, Osteen emphasizes having confidence in yourself. He writes, "Start thinking, feeling, and speaking positively about yourself. The Scripture says, 'Our faith is made effectual when we acknowledge everything good in us,' . . . Our faith is most effective when we acknowledge the good things that are in us. Declare affirmations such as 'I have a bright future. I am gifted. I am talented. People like me. I have the favor of God.'"[73] Osteen supports his instruction to declare such affirmations by focusing on the end of Philemon 6. This entire verse reads, "And I pray that the sharing of your faith may become effective for the full knowledge of every good thing that is in us for the sake of Christ." Note how Osteen only uses, or perhaps misuses, part of the verse to fit his own presuppositions. Osteen concludes that faith simply depends on one's own ability to locate the good things inside oneself, which he defines as talents, gifts, and the future.

Too often, Osteen does not accurately interpret Scripture and overlooks significant themes. In *It's Your Time*, he spends two chapters recounting the death and resurrection of Jesus Christ but never explains why Jesus had to die and be resurrected. In fact, Osteen makes no mention of sin until the very end of the book. Instead, almost unthinkably, Osteen compares the suffering of Jesus to the challenges that believers face in everyday life. He writes, "Before Jesus came to the resurrection, He endured the Garden of Gethsemane, the road to Golgotha, and death on the cross. Those were His biggest challenges. And they led to His greatest moment. Many times on the way to our dreams being fulfilled, we go through these same types of experiences."[74] Sadly, Osteen presents the death, burial, and resurrection of Christ as a paradigm for overcoming challenges and obstacles in life instead of exalting Christ as the substitutionary sacrifice for sin.

The Power of Words

As we have seen, a consistent theme in prosperity theology is the proper use of words. Osteen is no exception. In *Your Best Life Now*, he encourages, "Friend, there is a miracle in your mouth. If you want to change your world, start by changing your words. . . . If you'll learn how to speak the right words and keep the right attitude, God will turn that situation around."[75] According to Osteen, if you struggle, you boldly declare, "'Everything I put my hands to prospers and succeeds!' Friend, when you make those kinds of bold declarations, all heaven comes to attention to back up God's Word."[76] Osteen also instructs the reader to "use words to change your situation" because "with our words, we can prophesy our own future."[77]

**There is a miracle in your mouth.
If you want to change your world, start by changing your words.
. . . If you'll learn how to speak the right words and
keep the right attitude, God will turn that situation around.**
Joel Osteen

In one of his action points, Osteen suggests refreshing your self-image by speaking such words as "I am blessed; I am prosperous; I am healthy; I am continually growing wiser."[78] If you can talk to yourself the right way, you will "rise higher and see God's blessings and favor in a greater way."[79] Note that Osteen's belief in the power of words places people in control of their own destinies. In *It's Your Time* Osteen encourages his readers to declare positive thoughts in order to bring about good results. He writes, "When you sense it's your season, you need to declare it. Words have creative power. You need to hear it, and so does the enemy. You may not feel well, but it's good to announce: 'Health is coming my way. I will live and not die.' . . . Of course, it's important to think right. It's important to believe right. But something supernatural happens when we speak it out. . . . When you say of the Lord you are healthy, you are whole, you are free, you are blessed, you are prosperous—when you say it, God has promised He will do it."[80] Consciously or not, Osteen is simply reciting New Thought metaphysics. The Bible does not instruct believers to repeat phrases in order to control their thoughts. The Bible does, however, encourage believers to trust in God's sovereignty, to meditate upon His Word, and to use one's speech in order to encourage others.

Redefining the Gospel

On the very last page of *Your Best Life Now*, Osteen writes, "Are you at peace with God? A void exists in every person's heart that only God can fill. . . . Just say, 'Lord Jesus, I repent of my sins. I ask You to come into my heart. I make You my Lord and Savior.'"[81] This is the invitation that he gives at the end of each broadcast, and Lakewood Church reports significant numbers of people being saved. While such an invitation is commendable, as with the more mainstream proponents of the prosperity gospel, the question is, "Saved from what?" After reading Osteen's books, one might conclude that a person is saved from the possibility of a difficult life, rather than from one's sinful condition.

As Osteen explains in *Become a Better You*, "When we believe in God's Son, Jesus Christ, and *believe in ourselves*, that's when faith comes alive. When we believe we have what it takes, we focus on our possibilities."[82] In *It's Your Time* Osteen suggests, "When you're in difficult times, it's good to remind God what you've done. 'God, I kept my family in church. God, I've gone the extra mile to help others. I've given. I've served. I've been faithful.' In your own time of need you should call in all those seeds you've sown."[83] Contrary to Osteen's teaching here, biblical faith involves rejecting a self-righteous standard and recognizing that only Christ has the power to save. Osteen's focus on a person's possibilities contradicts Jesus' statement, "Apart from me you can do nothing" (John 15:5). Though ostensibly sincere, Osteen is teaching a false gospel. Those who follow Osteen's gospel will indeed experience their best life now because, tragically, they will die without having repented of sin and placing faith in the work and person of Jesus Christ.

In the chapter "Stop Listening to Accusing Voices" in *Become a Better You*, Osteen writes extensively about people's mistakes and how God views people. His position is that as long as you are doing your best and desiring to do what is right according to the Bible, God is pleased. He asserts that you should "take the pressure off yourself; give yourself the right to have some weaknesses and not to perform perfectly 100 percent of the time."[84] According to Osteen, what is important is that God knows your heart and, if you give your best effort, God will approve. If you make a mistake, then repent and move on. Why? Not because you have sinned against God but because you want God's favor. Osteen writes, "If you want to receive something good from God, come to Him humbly and with reverence, but come to Him in boldness. 'God, I've made mistakes, but I know You love me, and I'm asking for forgiveness; I'm receiving Your mercy.' Then go out expecting God's blessings and favor."[85]

Osteen's gospel, then, is that Jesus died in order to save man from a less than ideal life. Absent from his preaching is a well-defined concept of original sin, as well as a biblical explanation of the death of Jesus Christ on the cross. Of course, within prosperity theology these omissions make sense, for negative thoughts impact your ability to gain God's favor; thus, sin and the cross are omitted.

Redefining Humanity

Not surprisingly, Osteen holds an optimistic view of the goodness of people and their abilities. In fact, like Jakes, Osteen apparently believes that humans have the DNA of God. According to Osteen, inside each of us are seeds of greatness, and we are the seed of Almighty God. Since God paid the price for us, we are champions on the inside. How can we be assured of this fact? Osteen says, "It's in your blood."[86] Osteen believes that addictions and mind-sets get passed to the next generation literally through blood. If this is true, Osteen asks, "How much more can God's blessings, favor, and good habits be passed down through our blood?"[87]

Osteen claims that people can change by "thinking power thoughts."[88] If you exercise your authority, you can defeat hereditary disease. Osteen himself declares every day, "I will fulfill my destiny in good health."[89]

He believes that your actions are determinative for your descendants. He writes, "Get up every day and give it your best effort. If you will do that, not only will you rise higher and accomplish more, but God has promised that your seed, your family line for up to a thousand generations, is going to have the blessings and the favor of God—all because of the life that you've lived."[90] Once again, this approach is a works-based righteousness that eliminates God's grace and makes claims about God that simply are not true. God never promised unconditional blessing and favor to one's descendants. The basis of the blessing that God has promised is not your works or genetics but the life of Christ. It is true that you can and should influence your descendants and be an example, but, ultimately, your descendants will make their own decisions about Christ.

Theological Confusion

In his interviews on national television over the past few years, Osteen has failed to articulate a clear view of the gospel. For example, in a *60 Minutes* interview that aired in the fall of 2007, interviewer Byron Pitts perceptively commented, "To become a better you, you must be positive towards yourself, develop better relationships, embrace the place where you are. Not one mention of God in that. Not one mention of Jesus Christ in that." Osteen responded, "That's just my message. There is Scripture in there that backs it all up. But I feel like, Byron, I'm called to help people. . . . How do we walk out the Christian life? How do we live it? And these are principles that can help you. I mean, there's a lot better people qualified to say, 'Here's a book that is going to explain the Scriptures to you.' I don't think that's my gifting."[91] Byron Pitts's comments highlight a significant problem with Osteen's message—it is not centered on Christ. Osteen's answer also reveals a second problem; Osteen is preaching his own message.

In an interview with Osteen, Larry King asked why there are so few references to Scripture in *Your Best Life Now* until the very end of the book. Osteen answered, "It doesn't do a whole lot of it. My message, I wanted to reach the mainstream. We've reached the church audience. So I just try to, what I do is just try to teach practical principles. I may not bring the Scripture in until the end of my sermon and I might feel bad about that. Here's the thought. I talked yesterday about living to give. That's what a life should be about. I brought in at the end about some of the Scriptures that talk about that. But [the] same principle [is] in the book."[92]

Osteen's message of hope and lack of skill with the Scriptures emerge later in the Larry King interview. Larry King, wanting to know what happens to an unbeliever, asked, "What if you're Jewish or Muslim, you don't accept Christ at all?" Osteen responded vaguely, "You know, I'm very careful about saying who would and wouldn't go to heaven. I don't know." King pressed, "If you believe you have to believe in Christ[, then] they're wrong, aren't they?" Unable to evade the question, Osteen responded, "Well, I don't know if I believe they're wrong. I believe here's what the Bible teaches and from the Christian faith this is what I believe. But I just think that only God will judge a person's heart. I spent a lot of time in India with my father. I don't know all about their religion. But I know they love God. And I don't know. I've seen their sincerity. So I don't know. I know for me, and what the Bible teaches, I want to have a relationship with Jesus."[93] It is clear that Osteen does not understand that Jesus is the only way to God the Father (John 14:6).

In December of 2007, Chris Wallace on *Fox News Sunday*, asked Osteen in reference to Mitt Romney, if Mormons are true Christians. Osteen responded, "Well, in my mind they are. Mitt Romney has said that he believes in Christ as his Savior, and that's what I believe, so, you know, I'm not the one to judge the little details of it. So I believe they are." Wallace then asked, "So, for instance, when people start talking about Joseph Smith, the founder of the church, and the golden tablets in upstate New York, and God assumes the shape of a man, do you not get hung up in those theological issues?" Osteen answered, "I probably don't get hung up in them because I haven't really studied them or thought about them. And you know, I just try to let God be the judge of that. I mean, I don't know. I certainly can't say that I agree with everything that I've heard about it, but from what I've heard from Mitt, when he says that Christ is his Savior, to me that's a common bond."[94]

It is clear from these few interviews that Osteen neither understands Scriptures nor does he place Scripture in the center of his message. Furthermore, Osteen distorts the true gospel message and thereby misleads his followers. Joel Osteen is sincere and really wants to help people. Yet, good intentions do not excuse him from being held accountable for misleading people and preaching a false message.

SUMMARY POINTS

- Key historical figures in the prosperity gospel movement include E. W. Kenyon and Kenneth Hagin.
- Many contemporary prosperity gospel teachers are associated with the Word of Faith organization and/or the Trinity Broadcasting Network (TBN).
- The prosperity gospel is a broad movement, and there are many differences between the doctrines espoused by various prosperity gospel advocates.
- Like New Thought, the prosperity gospel movement is marked by several commonalities, including a distorted view of God, an elevation of mind over matter, an exalted view of people, a focus on attaining health and wealth, and an unorthodox view of salvation.
- Joel Osteen is an example of a contemporary soft-advocate of the prosperity gospel.

Chapter 3

The Errors of the Prosperity Gospel

All believers are theologians, for everyone has beliefs about God, moral issues, the church, and many other subjects. The question is whether each individual is a good or a bad theologian. Good theologians do not use Scripture to suit their purposes but rather allow Scripture to form their understanding of doctrine. Good theologians believe what accords with Scripture and compare all teachings with the Word of God. Bad theologians, however, use Scripture to justify their preconceived ideas instead of allowing the text to inform their beliefs—a practice often referred to as proof-texting. Obviously, incorrect theology will lead to and include incorrect beliefs about God, His Word, and His dealings with humanity. Bad theology can also lead to a host of practical problems across the doctrinal spectrum since ethics are essentially theology in action.

THE THEOLOGY OF THE PROSPERITY GOSPEL

It is the contention of this book that despite the good intentions of some of its proponents—especially among the soft advocates—the prosperity gospel is constructed upon faulty theology. As will be argued in this chapter, many of the doctrines of prosperity gospel teachers are erroneous. While it is beyond the scope of this book to examine all the doctrines associated with the prosperity gospel, several fundamental doctrines can be examined in order to illustrate the nature and extent of the theological errors within this movement. The specific teachings of the prosperity gospel that this chapter will focus on are the gospel, faith, the atonement, the Abrahamic covenant, the mind, prayer, the Bible, and giving.

Prosperity Theology and the Gospel

The biblical gospel is the core of the Christian message. Rightly preached, rightly shared, and rightly understood, the gospel can bring life to the unregenerate heart. The gospel wrongly preached, wrongly shared, and wrongly understood can lead the faithful astray or—even worse—leave the blind in their fallen state. With life and death in the balance, believers ought to be passionate about the gospel. Pastor C. J. Mahaney writes, "If there's anything in life that we should be passionate about, it's the gospel. And I don't mean passionate only about sharing it with others. I mean passionate about thinking about it, dwelling on it, rejoicing in it, allowing it to color the way we look at the world. Only one thing can be of first importance to each of us. And only the gospel ought to be."[1] To be passionate about the gospel, believers must both experience and understand it. This invites the question, "How do you define the gospel?" Without a clear understanding of the gospel, you will not be equipped to evaluate the prosperity gospel or to identify the errors of those within this movement.

When we think of the gospel, we rightly think of the offer of salvation and what it means. Paul defines and explains the gospel in 1 Corinthians 15:3–4. The apostle says, "For I delivered to you as of first importance what I also received: that Christ died for our sins in accordance with the Scriptures, that he was buried, that he was raised on the third day in accordance with the Scriptures." The apostle further crystallizes the core elements of the gospel in Romans 3:21–26 and 2 Corinthians 5:11–21. There are several noteworthy elements in these passages. First, God is holy and perfectly righteous (see Rom. 3:21); yet, in His mercy and grace, the Lord chose to save rebellious, sinful people (see Rom. 3:25). Second, every person has sinned against a holy God and deserves hell (see Rom. 3:23). No one can meet God's standards of perfection. No one is good enough to merit God's grace, and everyone is under God's wrath against sin, as well as His judgment. Third, the triune God sent Jesus to earth to accomplish redemption (see Rom. 3:24–25). Jesus, being both fully God and fully man, lived a perfect, sinless life in obedience to His Father. He lived the life that we could not. Fourth, Jesus died willingly on the cross in the place of sinners. In this loving act, He became sin for us (see 2 Cor. 5:21). Jesus satisfied the wrath of God against sin, the wrath and judgment that people deserved (see Rom. 3:25). Jesus is our substitute and with His death on the cross, He took the punishment for our sins. Fifth, God was reconciling humanity to Himself (see 2 Cor. 5:18). The debt of sin was canceled and trespasses are not counted against those who believe. As Paul writes, "We have redemption, the forgiveness of sins" (Col. 1:14). Sixth, God raised Jesus from the dead for our justification (see Rom. 4:25). Through the resurrection, then, God demonstrated that He approved of Jesus' sacrifice and thereby ensured salvation for all who believe.

Certainly much more could be said about the gospel, yet what is sure is that Jesus—His life, death, burial, and resurrection—is central to the gospel. Without Jesus, without the cross, and without the resurrection, there is no gospel. The famous nineteenth-century pastor Charles Spurgeon placed Christ at the heart of the gospel. He preached, "The heart of the gospel is redemption, and the essence of redemption is the substitutionary sacrifice of Christ. They who preach this truth preach the gospel in whatever else they may be mistaken; but they who preach not the atonement, whatever else they declare, have missed the soul and substance of the divine message."[2]

After arriving at a working definition of the gospel, the next question is, "How does one become righteous before God?" Again, Scripture provides a clear answer. First, a person must repent of sin (see Acts 17:30; 26:20). This means recognizing the seriousness of sin, confessing sin before God, and asking for forgiveness. Repentance is more than being sorry; it is forsaking whatever you trust in for security and self-worth and turning, in faith, toward Jesus Christ. Second, that person must place faith in Jesus and His work on the cross on behalf of humanity. Paul repeatedly called people to confess Jesus as Lord and to believe the truth about Jesus: that He died, was buried, and rose again (see Rom. 10:10–11; 1 Cor. 15:3–4). The apostle Paul is clear that salvation is by God's grace alone through faith alone in Jesus Christ alone (see Eph. 2:8–9; Rom. 3:24). People do not earn God's grace and do not deserve God's grace. Salvation is a free gift to all who believe, and God's promise is that all who believe will be saved. Christians are new creatures created in Jesus Christ, now able to stand before God without condemnation. Believers are free from the power of sin and through the Holy Spirit are able to please God. This is the good news of the gospel. In his pamphlet *The Way to Salvation*, nineteenth-century pastor J. C. Ryle summarized the gospel as follows:

> Where must a man go for pardon? Where is forgiveness to be found? There is a way both sure and plain, and into that way I desire to guide every inquirer's feet. That way is simply to trust in the Lord Jesus Christ as your Savior. It is to cast your soul with all its sins, unreservedly on Christ—to cease completely from any dependence on your own works or doings, either in whole or in part—and to rest on no other work but Christ's work—no other righteousness but Christ's righteousness, no other merit but Christ's merit as your ground of hope. Take this course—and you are a pardoned soul.[3]

Though salvation is a free gift, it comes with demands. If rightly understood, salvation costs people everything. Listen to Jesus' words to the Pharisees, "If anyone would come after me, let him deny himself and take up his cross and follow me. For whoever would save his life will lose it, but whoever loses his life for my sake and the gospel's will save it" (Mark 8:34–35). Jesus never promised His followers an easy life. In fact, He told them to count the cost and be ready to suffer and die for their trust in Him. A biblical perspective on suffering will be explored further in chapter 4.

If believed, the gospel saves people from death, judgment, and hell. This is certainly a result of the gospel, but it is not the end of the gospel in the believer's life. Believers need the power of the gospel every day to live for Christ. Too often, Christians tend to think of the gospel only in terms of salvation for the lost. Obviously, unbelievers need to hear the gospel in order to repent and believe, but viewing this as the extent of the gospel is to fail to realize that the gospel saves from the power of sin. Followers of Christ need to preach the gospel to themselves every day. Unless Christians do so, they will fall into a works-based scheme of self-sanctification. The gospel, through the Holy Spirit, helps to produce Christlike character and growth in holiness. In his work *Gospel-Driven Sanctification,* author Jerry Bridges reflects on the importance of the gospel. He notes:

> Christians need to hear the gospel all of their lives because it is the gospel that continues to remind us that our day-to-day acceptance with the Father is not based on what we do for God but upon what Christ did for us in his sinless life and sin-bearing death. . . . We stand before God today as righteous as we ever will be, even in heaven, because he has clothed us with the righteousness of his Son. Therefore, I don't have to perform to be accepted by God. Now I am free to obey him and serve him because I am already accepted in Christ (see Rom. 8:1). My driving motivation now is not guilt but gratitude.[4]

Bridges says that Christians should practice spiritual disciplines such as praying, reading the Bible, and being in church. Yet, believers do not serve, pray, or read to be more loved by God; rather, they serve, pray, and read because they are loved by God. The gospel communicates this truth and aids believers in depending on Christ to grow in holiness.

How does the message of the biblical gospel compare to that of the prosperity gospel? As suggested in the previous chapter, there are several theological problems with the prosperity gospel. For example, advocates of the prosperity gospel marginalize key components of the biblical gospel, such as Jesus, the cross, God's judgment, and the sinful estate of humanity. If Jesus is left out of the gospel, then there is no gospel. If the cross is left out of the gospel, then there is no gospel. If God's judgment against sin is left out of the gospel, then there is no gospel. If humanity's sin is left out of the gospel, then there is no gospel.

Consider the message of prosperity gospel advocate Joel Osteen. On the television show *60 Minutes*, Byron Pitts summarized what he perceived to be the emphases within Osteen's message. Pitts commented, "God is a loving, forgiving God who will reward believers with health, wealth and happiness. It's the centerpiece of every sermon. . . . To become a better you, you must be positive towards yourself, develop better relationships, embrace the place where you are. Not one mention of God in that. Not one mention of Jesus Christ in that."[5] Osteen replied, "That's just my message."[6] This is a remarkable statement for an evangelical pastor in light of the apostle Paul's call to preach Jesus Christ as Lord and Him crucified (see 1 Cor. 2:1–2). Michael Horton, professor of systematic theology at Westminster Seminary California, observes, "It is not obvious that Christ—at least his incarnation, obedient life, atoning death, and justifying and life-giving resurrection—is necessary at all in Osteen's scheme."[7] The prosperity message can be and is often preached without Jesus.

Additionally, the prosperity gospel turns the gospel of Christ into a human-focused religion. Note that in His ministry Jesus reserved His most scathing words for the religious leaders who turned the biblical gospel into a man-made religion. In the prosperity gospel, believers dictate the terms of their lives to God as they seek after health, wealth, and other forms of personal flourishing. The thinking appears to be "I do good things, and I obey God, and I try my best for the purpose of getting things from God." The prosperity gospel teaches believers to depend on their own works, thoughts, and efforts in order to succeed in life. The biblical gospel shows people that they are sinners and must rely on Jesus' work on the cross in order to become accepted in the Beloved (see Eph. 1:5–6).

The prosperity gospel does not point people toward Christ. Instead, it points them to the lust of the eyes, the lust of the flesh, and the pride of life (see 1 John 2:15–17). For the prosperity faithful, hope rests in accomplishments, dreams, money, and accolades. This is a superficial, temporary, and shallow understanding of the biblical message of hope.

> **There are certain laws governing prosperity revealed in God's Word. Faith causes them to function.**
> Kenneth Copeland

The Prosperity Gospel and Faith

Another area of prosperity theology that merits investigation is its doctrine of faith. While prosperity teachers talk about faith, their understanding of what faith is and what faith accomplishes differs from the traditional, biblical understanding of faith. Whereas orthodox Christianity understands faith to be "trust in the person of Jesus Christ, the truth of His teaching, and the redemptive work He accomplished at Calvary,"[8] prosperity teachers espouse quite a different doctrine. In his book *The Laws of Prosperity*, Kenneth Copeland writes that "faith is a spiritual force, a spiritual energy, a spiritual power. It is this force of faith which makes the laws of the spirit world function. . . . There are certain laws governing prosperity revealed in God's Word. Faith causes them to function."[9] This is obviously a faulty, if not heretical, understanding of faith. Later in the same book Copeland claims, "If you make up your mind . . . that you are willing to live in divine prosperity and abundance . . . divine prosperity will come to pass in your life. You have exercised your faith."[10] According to prosperity theology, faith is not a theocentric act of the will, stemming from God; rather it is an anthropocentric spiritual force, directed at God.

To believe the gospel is to believe in Jesus and His power. It is to trust in God's revealed grace. There are numerous examples of Jesus healing in response to great displays of faith. Consider the following:

- A centurion came to Jesus to seek healing for a paralyzed servant who was at his home. After Jesus said that He would come to the home and heal the servant, the centurion responded, "Lord, I am not worthy to have you come under my roof, but only say the word, and my servant will be healed" (Matt. 8:8). Jesus marveled and said, "Truly, I tell you, with no one in Israel have I found such faith" (Matt. 8:10). In this instance, Jesus recognized the centurion's faith—that is, his trust in the promised Messiah to heal his servant, and even to do so from a distance.

- A woman suffering from bleeding for twelve years thought that if she just touched Jesus' clothing, she would be healed. She believed that Jesus had supernatural power to heal. He said, "Take heart, daughter; your faith has made you well" (Matt. 9:22). Who or what was the object of her faith? It was Jesus and His ability to perform the miraculous. Faith in Jesus focuses on His ability to accomplish the impossible.

- The parents of a demon-possessed boy came to Jesus and said, "If you can do anything, take pity on us and help us!" Jesus replied, "'If you can'! All things are possible for one who believes" (Mark 9:23). Based upon the parents' declaration of faith—that is, their educated belief in Him—Jesus healed their son.

These narratives illustrate the necessity of faith for healing; yet the faith required is always in Jesus. Contrary to the teaching of the prosperity gospel, believers are never commanded to have faith in words or their own powers. Joel Osteen encourages people to use such phrases as "I am blessed; I am prosperous; I am healthy; I am continually growing wiser."[11] Osteen and others think that a person has to amass the proper amount of faith in order to move God on his or her behalf. Such a belief is akin to having faith in oneself or, perhaps, having faith in faith, as opposed to having faith in God. Kenneth Hagin, author of the tellingly titled *Having Faith in Your Faith*, instructs his followers to declare, "Faith in my faith."[12] Teachers such as Hagin believe that when the right amount of faith is manifested, God grants healing and blessings. This is because God is bound by the universal spiritual laws that have been established. Faith is a magic formula that enables believers to obtain what they desire.

By way of contrast, consider the example of Job, certainly a man of great faith (see James 5:11). Job suffered greatly, losing his children, servants, health, and livelihood, yet he still trusted in God. He refused to curse God and instead responded, "Naked I came from my mother's womb, and naked shall I return. The LORD gave, and the LORD has taken away; blessed be the name of the LORD" (Job 1:21). After enduring the advice of his friends, Job declared, "Though he [God] slay me, I will hope in him" (Job 13:15). Here is a man who had great faith in God, so great that God allowed him to be tested by Satan. It seems ludicrous to argue, as prosperity gospel advocate Joyce Meyer does, that Job's negative thoughts brought disaster upon him.[13] Job demonstrated genuine faith in God despite pain, sorrow, and confusion. The narrative of Job illustrates the fact that biblical faith is not a force, but it is confidence in God.

The Prosperity Gospel and the Atonement

Another area in which many advocates of the prosperity gospel err is their doctrine of the atonement. Theologian Ken Sarles summarized the prosperity view of the atonement: "The prosperity gospel claims that both physical healing and financial prosperity have been provided for in the atonement."[14] This seems to be an accurate observation in light of teacher Kenneth Copeland's comment that "the basic principle of the Christian life is to know that God put our sin, sickness, disease, sorrow, grief, and poverty on Jesus at Calvary."[15] This misunderstanding of the atonement stems from two foundational errors.

First, many who hold to prosperity theology have a fundamental misconception of the life and ministry of Christ. For example, almost unbelievably, prosperity gospel teacher John Avanzini proclaimed, "Jesus had a nice house, a big house,"[16] "Jesus was handling big money,"[17] and that Christ even "wore designer clothes."[18] It is easy to see how such a warped view of the life of Jesus could lead to an equally warped misconception of His death.

A second error of prosperity theology that contributes to a faulty view of the atonement is a misinterpretation of 2 Corinthians 8:9. Without exception, this is the verse to which prosperity teachers appeal in order to support their understanding of the death of Christ. The verse reads, "For you know the grace of our Lord Jesus Christ, that though he was rich, yet for your sake he became poor, so that you by his poverty might become rich" (2 Cor. 8:9). Paul is not teaching that Christ died on the cross for the purpose of increasing one's material net worth. In fact, he is actually teaching the exact opposite. Contextually, it is clear that Paul was teaching the Corinthians that since Christ accomplished so much for them through the atonement, they ought to empty themselves of their riches in service of the Savior. This is why just five verses later Paul urges the Corinthians to give their wealth to their needy brothers, writing that "your abundance at the present time should supply their need . . . that there may be fairness" (2 Cor. 8:14).

Prosperity theology also teaches that Jesus' death provides for physical healing. Two key passages mentioned in support of this view are Isaiah 53:5, which reads, "and with his stripes we are healed," and 1 Peter 2:24, where Peter writes, "By his wounds you have been healed." Joyce Meyer claims that believers do not have to endure sickness because Jesus provided healing on the cross. In one of her physical healing confessions, she writes, "By His stripes I was healed. Healing belongs to me. I was healed two thousand years ago by the stripes Jesus bore. By His stripes I was healed. I'm not trying to get healing; I've already got my healing, because by His stripes I was healed!"[19]

If immediate physical healing is promised in the atonement, then believers should either not be sick at all or be healed when they exercise faith. Kenneth Hagin argues, "Don't ever tell anyone sickness is the will of God for us. It isn't! Healing and health are the will of God for mankind. If sickness were the will of God, heaven would be filled with sickness and disease."[20] According to prosperity teachers, the cure for sickness is to have a positive outlook—thinking and saying the right words. Exercise your faith in those words to combat your disease and keep building up your faith to remove the sickness. Joyce Meyer proclaims,

I have faith, for I am a believer. I believe I receive my healing, and my faith makes me whole. . . . The power that raised Christ from the dead is at work in me. My faith puts that power into active operation in my body. Disease has no choice. There is no chance for its survival in my body. . . . That power is flowing in me and makes me whole. I am free. I am entirely free from sickness and disease. I am whole. I believe I have received my healing, and my faith has made me whole![21]

If healing does not occur, the problem is your lack of faith. Robert Tilton guarantees that God will "always heal on faith."[22]

The power that raised Christ from the dead is at work in me. My faith puts that power into active operation in my body.

Joyce Meyer

Does the atonement include physical healing for the believer today? A closer look at the context of Isaiah 53:5 indicates that the healing cited by the prophet is spiritual in nature—that is, the remission of sin. Isaiah 53:4–5 reads, "Surely he has borne our griefs and carried our sorrows; yet we esteemed him stricken, smitten by God, and afflicted. But he was wounded for our transgressions; he was crushed for our iniquities; upon him was the chastisement that brought us peace, and with his stripes we are healed." The meaning is clear in these verses: through His death Christ atoned for believers' sins.[23] First Peter 2:24 furthers clarifies the meaning of Isaiah 53:4–5. Peter writes, "He himself bore our sins in his body on the tree, that we might die to sin and live to righteousness. By his wounds you have been healed."

Prosperity teachers create problems when they argue for physical healing in the atonement. Such a claim assumes that sickness is itself sin or the result of an individual's sin, but this is not always true. Sickness, in and of itself, is not sin. Certainly sin can induce sickness, but this is not always (or even usually) the case. Note that incorrectly connecting sin and sickness is the mistake that Jesus' disciples made, and Christ confronts, in John 9:1–7. In this passage the apostles ask Jesus if a certain man was blind from birth due to his sin or his parents' sin. Jesus replies, "It was not that this man sinned, or his parents, but that the works of God might be displayed in him" (John 9:3).

Another problem with connecting physical healing with the atonement is that physical restoration must be guaranteed for followers of Christ. If immediate spiritual healing is guaranteed for all who repent and believe, then why would not immediate physical healing be guaranteed? The fact that physical healing is not manifest among followers of the prosperity gospel becomes problematic. In his analysis of the prosperity gospel, Hank Hanegraaff cites this inconsistency as he observes, "If one does not have enough faith to make oneself well, it follows that he cannot have enough faith to be saved."[24]

Prosperity teachers not only misinterpret the atonement, but they also abuse the atonement of Christ by stressing the benefits of the cross while ignoring its claims. The cross becomes little more than a means to an end: Jesus died for your sins so that you can be prosperous and healthy. This contrasts with the biblical message that believers must take up their cross daily and die to self in order to live for Christ (see Matt. 16:24). The cross demands that followers of Christ make sacrifices for the sake of the kingdom of God and exalt God rather than themselves. The prosperity gospel distorts the meaning of the atonement and, therefore, is not the gospel at all.

The Prosperity Gospel and the Abrahamic Covenant

In Genesis 12:1–3, God promised to make Abraham a great nation, to bless him, and to make his name great. Theologians refer to this event as the Abrahamic covenant, and it is a foundational component of orthodox Christian theology. A survey of the literature produced by the advocates of the prosperity gospel reveals that the Abrahamic covenant is an important component of prosperity theology too.[25] While it is good that prosperity theologians recognize that much of Scripture records the fulfillment of the Abrahamic covenant, many prosperity theologians hold to an unorthodox, incorrect view of the Abrahamic covenant itself, especially the modern application of the covenant.[26]

Researcher Edward Pousson best states the prosperity view on the application of the Abrahamic covenant when he writes, "Christians are Abraham's spiritual children and heirs to the blessings of faith. . . . This Abrahamic inheritance is unpacked primarily in terms of material entitlements."[27] In other words, according to the prosperity gospel, the primary purpose of the Abrahamic covenant was for God to bless Abraham materially and to make him successful. Advocates of the prosperity gospel reason that since believers are now Abraham's spiritual children, they consequently have inherited the material blessings of the covenant.

This idea of covenant is vital to the prosperity gospel. For prosperity teachers, a covenant is akin to an inviolable contract with God. This is good news for the prosperity faithful, because God is obligated to come through if a believer exercises faith in the covenant. Paula White exclaims, "God's Word is full of covenants for our lives. All God's benefits of the blessing, such as healing, deliverance, salvation, financial increase, wholeness, and fulfillment, are available because of covenant. . . . We receive God's promises by the covenant, and we activate the blessing of God through our faith in the covenant."[28] Similarly, prosperity teacher Kenneth Copeland writes, "Since God's Covenant has been established and prosperity is a provision of this Covenant, you need to realize that prosperity belongs to you now!"[29] God made an agreement with Abraham, and, when accessed by faith, the blessings are passed on to Abraham's spiritual children in the form of material blessings.

Creflo Dollar has the same view of covenants, specifically the Abrahamic covenant, as do White and Copeland. In a sermon on Genesis 12:1–3, Dollar emphasizes that Abraham went down to Egypt during a time of famine, but that he returned to the Promised Land with cattle, silver, and gold. He tells his congregation that Abraham's riches can be attributed to God's blessing on his life. Then Dollar jumps to the New Testament and, focusing on Galatians 3:13–14, argues that this blessing is available to Abraham's seed through the death of Jesus. Dollar concludes, "God has to prosper you because of the covenant He has established with you."[30] Notice how Dollar portrays the covenant in terms of material wealth and emphasizes God's obligation to provide increase.

Joel Osteen's teaching on the Abrahamic covenant is similar to that of other prosperity gospel advocates. In his best-selling book *Become a Better You*, Osteen rightly notes that believers are spiritual heirs of Abraham. Osteen's application of the Abrahamic covenant, however, goes awry as he writes, "I love the Scripture that says, 'If we belong to Christ, we are Abraham's seed, and heirs according to the promise.' That means we can all experience the blessings of Abraham. If you study Abraham's record, you'll discover that he was prosperous, healthy, and lived a long, productive life. Even though he didn't always make the best choices, he enjoyed God's blessings and favor."[31]

In reference to certain prosperity teachers' view of the Abrahamic covenant, prosperity gospel critic Harvey Cox writes, "Through the crucifixion of Christ, Christians have inherited all the promises made to Abraham, and these include both spiritual and material well-being."[32] To support this claim, prosperity teachers such as White, Copeland, Dollar, and Osteen often appeal to Galatians 3:14, in which Paul writes that the crucifixion occurred "so that in Christ Jesus the blessing of Abraham might come to the Gentiles." Yet prosperity teachers ignore the second half of the verse, which reads, ". . . so that we might receive the promised Spirit through faith." In this verse Paul is clearly reminding the Galatians of the spiritual blessing of salvation, not the material blessing of wealth.

Another problem with prosperity teachers' view of the Abrahamic covenant is the claim that the conduit through which believers receive Abraham's blessings is faith. This completely ignores the orthodox understanding that the Abrahamic covenant was an unconditional covenant.[33] The blessings of the Abrahamic covenant were not contingent upon one man's obedience. Therefore, even if the Abrahamic covenant did apply to Christians, all believers would already be experiencing the material blessings regardless of prosperity theology.

This error seems to stem from prosperity teachers' confusion of biblical covenants with modern-day contracts. A divine covenant is not performance-based. If Abraham failed, God would have fulfilled His promise because God cannot lie (see Heb. 6:18). A contract, on the other hand, implies services and benefits rendered to both parties. Both sides have something to offer each other in the contract. If one side fails to deliver, then the contract is broken. While the contract suits the prosperity gospel's purposes, it fails to reflect the biblical idea of covenant.[34]

The Prosperity Gospel and the Mind

The prosperity gospel encourages believers to make positive verbal and mental confessions concerning objects of personal desire. According to prosperity teachers, the faithful should focus their thoughts and words on increased finances, better health, success in the workplace, and beneficial personal relationships. Of course, biblically speaking, there is nothing inherently wrong with desiring prosperity; yet, if personal flourishing begins to consume one's thoughts, such desires have become idolatrous.

Contrast what is emphasized in prosperity theology with what Paul instructs the Philippian church to dwell on: "Finally, brothers, whatever is true, whatever is honorable, whatever is just, whatever is pure, whatever is lovely, whatever is commendable, if there is any excellence, if there is anything worthy of praise, think about these things" (Phil. 4:8). Notice that Paul does not tell his readers to focus their minds on larger homes, nicer cars, perfect health, and occupational promotions. Instead the apostle encourages his readers to contemplate truth, God's Word, and God Himself. Whatever is worthy of worship, or upholds the righteous standards of a holy God, demands the attention of God's people. Furthermore, Paul tells the believers in Colossae, "Set your minds on things that are above, not on things that are on earth" (Col. 3:2).

God instructs believers to protect their minds because a mind filled with God's Word will desire the things of God. Does the prosperity gospel cause its followers to focus more on Christ or on the things of this world? With the steady mantra of being successful and obtaining wealth, the prosperity gospel encourages believers to focus on themselves. Compare the prosperity gospel's emphasis on material success to the apostle John's warning, "Do not love the world or the things in the world. If anyone loves the world, the love of the Father is not in him. For all that is in the world— the desires of the flesh and the desires of the eyes and pride in possessions— is not from the Father but is from the world" (1 John 2:15–16). The biblical mandate is for believers to take their cues from the Bible rather than the world. This is not to suggest that Christians cannot desire personal success, but such a desire cannot be the ultimate goal of a believer's life.

We know that our thoughts are important, but what about our words? Do they matter? Do they have creative power? Prosperity gospel teachers stress that there is power in our words. In support of their claim, they quote verses such as Proverbs 18:21, "Death and life are in the power of the tongue." Yet, a look at the full context of this verse sheds more light on its meaning. Proverbs 18:20–21 reads, "From the fruit of a man's mouth his stomach is satisfied; he is satisfied by the yield of his lips. Death and life are in the power of the tongue, and those who love it will eat its fruits." Old Testament scholar Duane Garrett writes, "The purpose of these verses is to warn against being too much in love with one's own words. One should recognize the power of words and use them with restraint. Voicing one's own views, here ironically described as eating the fruit of the tongue, can be an addictive habit with dangerous results."[35] Therefore, this verse does not suggest that words have creative power, but rather that words can have both positive and negative effects upon people. As the Bible exhorts elsewhere, then, use your tongue wisely (see James 3:1–12).

The Prosperity Gospel and Prayer

Prosperity gospel preachers often note that we "have not because we ask not" (see James 4:2). They encourage believers to pray for personal success in all areas of life. Certainly personal success is not an inherently inappropriate prayer request, but the prosperity gospel's overemphasis on people turns prayer into a tool that believers can use to obtain their desires from God. Within prosperity theology, people—rather than

God—become the focal point of prayer. Curiously, prosperity preachers often ignore the second half of James's teaching on prayer, which reads, "You ask and do not receive, because you ask wrongly, to spend it on your passions" (James 4:3). God does not answer selfish requests that do not honor His name.

When we pray, believing that we have already received what we are praying, God has no choice but to make our prayers come to pass.
Creflo Dollar

In regard to the power of prayer, Creflo Dollar writes, "When we pray, believing that we have already received what we are praying, God has no choice but to make our prayers come to pass. . . . It is a key to getting results as a Christian. . . . We must not allow religion or tradition to blind us to the truth of what prayer really is."[36] Commenting on the prosperity that is available to believers through prayer, Dollar asks, "How can someone pray for healing when they do not know God wants them to be healed? How can we believe God for an increase in our finances if we do not know God wants us to prosper? The truth is—we cannot."[37] In Dollar's estimation, the faithful must believe that God will prosper and heal, and then pray in order to get results. Compared with biblical examples of prayer, Dollar's view of prayer seems self-centered. In his analysis of the doctrine of prayer within the prosperity movement, John MacArthur writes, "Teaching that claims we can demand things of God is spiritual justification for self-indulgence. It perverts prayer and takes the Lord's name in vain. It is unbiblical, ungodly, and is not directed by the Holy Spirit."[38]

While prosperity teachers talk about prayer, they undermine the biblical teaching on prayer. Scripture teaches that prayer is a means of fellowship with God and is an act of worship. Furthermore, prayer is asking that God's will be done; not that our will be fulfilled. Prayer focuses on God and His glory. This is central to Jesus' model prayer, the so-called Lord's Prayer. In this passage, Jesus teaches His followers how to pray, saying, "Pray then like this: 'Our Father in heaven, hallowed be your name. Your kingdom come, your will be done, on earth as it is in heaven. Give us this day our daily bread, and forgive us our debts, as we also have forgiven our debtors. And lead us not into temptation, but deliver us from evil'" (Matt. 6:9–13). Notice that Jesus' model for prayer begins with God, His character, His name, His honor, His kingdom, and His will and purposes. After reverently approaching God, the believer requests provision for the day, pardon for sins, and protection from temptation. Noticeably absent are requests for incredible personal flourishing.

The apostle Paul also provides several examples of prayer. Writing to the church in Ephesus, Paul prays "that the God of our Lord Jesus Christ, the Father of glory, may give you a spirit of wisdom and of revelation in the knowledge of him, having the eyes of your hearts enlightened, that you may know what is the hope to which he has called you, what are the riches of his glorious inheritance in the saints" (Eph. 1:17–18). The apostle prays that God will grant believers wisdom and knowledge so that they might know God and possess genuine hope. This prayer encourages the church to realize, by God's grace, what they have in Christ Jesus.

Later in Paul's letter to the Ephesians, he prays to the Father that "according to the riches of his glory he may grant you to be strengthened with power through his Spirit in your inner being, so that Christ may dwell in your hearts through faith—that you, being rooted and grounded in love, may have strength to comprehend with all the saints what is the breadth and length and height and depth, and to know the love of Christ that surpasses knowledge, that you may be filled with all the fullness of God" (Eph. 3:16–19). Paul's concern is that the believers be strengthened to know Christ and His love. Jesus and Paul are not obsessed with praying for material goods. Why should they be? Jesus told His followers that the Father already knows what they need and not to worry about such things (see Matt. 6:25–34). Rather, Christians are to "seek first the kingdom of God and his righteousness, and all these things will be added to you" (Matt. 6:33).

Certainly we should make all our requests known to God (see Phil. 4:6), but the prosperity gospel focuses so much on people's desires that it can lead us to pray selfish, shallow, superficial prayers that do not bring God glory. Furthermore, when coupled with the prosperity doctrine of faith, the teaching about prayer encourages people to try manipulating God to get what they want—indeed, a futile task. This is far removed from praying to God to see His will accomplished.

The Prosperity Gospel and the Bible

The hermeneutics—that is, the method of Bible interpretation—of some within the prosperity movement leaves much to be desired. In discussing the prosperity teachers, theologian Ken Sarles writes that their "method of interpreting the biblical text is highly subjective and arbitrary. Bible verses are quoted in abundance without attention to grammatical indicators, semantic nuances, or literary and historical context. The result is a set of ideas and principles based on distortion of textual meaning."[39] A survey of the volumes of literature produced by the prosperity teachers yields numerous examples of such misinterpretation, several of which have been documented in the previous and present chapter. While a comprehensive analysis of the hermeneutics of the prosperity gospel falls beyond the scope of this brief volume, for illustrative purposes we choose one verse as an example—3 John 2.[40]

In 3 John 2, the apostle John writes, "Beloved, I pray that you may prosper in all things and be in health, just as your soul prospers" (3 John 2 NKJV). Prosperity teachers interpret this verse to mean that God wants all believers to "prosper in all things." The late Oral Roberts, one of the founders of the prosperity gospel movement, claimed that at the beginning of his ministry, during a time of search for direction, God miraculously led him to 3 John 2, which he understood as a revelation of the prosperity gospel.[41] Another teacher who has built his ministry around 3 John 2 is Kenneth Copeland. Author Kenneth Kantzer notes that "Copeland misinterprets this [verse] as a universal promise,"[42] and writer Bruce Barron remarks that "the Copelands [Kenneth and Gloria] use these words so often that they appear to be the key verse of their ministry."[43] A careful study of 3 John 2, however, reveals that the apostle John is not teaching what has become known as the prosperity gospel.

Those who use 3 John 2 to support the prosperity gospel are committing two crucial errors, the first contextual and the second grammatical. First, contextually, one should note that John's purpose in writing 3 John 2 was not to teach doctrine; rather, he was simply opening his letter with a greeting. This is not to say that doctrine cannot be derived from nondoctrinal passages, for all Scripture is profitable for doctrine. Yet we must be sensitive to the original author's intent. The claim that 3 John 2 teaches the doctrine of prosperity ought to be regarded as suspect at best.

Second, one should note the meaning of the word *prosperity* as it occurs in this verse. The Greek term translated "prosperity," which is used only four times in Scripture, does not connote prosperity in the sense of gaining material possessions. Rather, the word means "to grant a prosperous expedition and expeditious journey," or "to lead by a direct and easy way."[44] The wording of modern translations such as the New International Version and English Standard Version reflect this nuance of the word. The New International Version translates 3 John 2, "Dear friend, I pray that you may enjoy good health and that all may go well with you, even as your soul is getting along well." Similarly, the English Standard Version reads, "Beloved, I pray that all may go well with you and that you may be in good health, as it goes well with your soul." Those who understand 3 John 2 to teach prosperity theology are misinterpreting the text.

Prosperity Theology and Giving

As mentioned in the previous chapter, one of the most prominent characteristics of prosperity theologians is their seeming fixation with the act of giving. Students of the prosperity gospel are urged to give generously, but a closer examination of the theology behind the encouragement to give reveals that the prosperity gospel's emphasis on giving is built on anything but philanthropic motives.

As noted earlier, Gloria Copeland claims, "Give $10 and receive $1,000; give $1,000 and receive $100,000. . . . In short, Mark 10:30 is a very good deal."[45] Yet, does Jesus promise an investment program with incredible financial returns? Mark 10:29–30 records Jesus saying, "Truly, I say to you, there is no one who has left house or brothers or sisters or mother or father or children or lands, for my sake and for the gospel, who will not receive a hundredfold now in this time, houses and brothers and sisters and mothers and children and lands, with persecutions, and in the age to come eternal life." What is the hundredfold return? The passage itself answers the question: houses, relatives, and lands with persecutions. In other words, when one leaves his current community in order to follow Jesus, he will become part of a new society comprised of believers, wherever he lives. The key to this interpretation is located in Mark 3 where Jesus addresses the question of genuine family. With His family outside the house in which He was preaching, Jesus looks around the group and says, "Here are my mother and my brothers! For whoever does the will of God, he is my brother and my sister and mother" (Mark 3:34–35). The hundredfold refers clearly to the family of believers.

Additionally, prosperity teachers often promote a give-to-get mentality. All believers need to do is sow a seed of faith—that is, donate money to the ministry—and God will bless their marriages, finances, or wherever other help is desired. Within the prosperity system, the goal in giving is ultimately to serve oneself instead of others. T. D. Jakes's appeal to his listeners is typical:

Remember, no need is too big for God. Maybe you need a miracle in your marriage. God can put it back together again. You could be facing unbelievable financial challenges; God can provide a supernatural increase. God knows where you need your miracle harvest, and now is the time to sow your Miracle Faith Seed. Even if you've already shared a gift, you still have time to increase your blessing during this miracle season of sowing. Take a moment to do two things: First, write your most urgent prayer request on the reply form and send it to me so I may join you in praying for your miracle harvest! Second, take a moment to sow the most generous miracle faith seed you can.[46]

The prosperity gospel's doctrine of giving is built on faulty motives. Whereas Jesus taught His disciples to "lend, expecting nothing in return" (Luke 6:35), prosperity theologians teach their disciples to give because they will get a great return.

CONCLUSION

The prosperity gospel is built upon a faulty understanding of (1) the gospel; (2) biblical teaching on faith; (3) the atonement; (4) the Abrahamic covenant; (5) biblical teaching about the mind; (6) biblical teaching about prayer; (7) biblical interpretation; and (8) biblical teaching on giving. One reason summarizes why the prosperity gospel is a wayward gospel: it has a faulty view of the relationship between God and humanity. Simply put, if the prosperity gospel is correct, grace becomes obsolete, God becomes irrelevant, and "man is the measure of all things." Whether it is the gospel, faith, the atonement, the Abrahamic covenant, the mind, prayer, Bible interpretation, or giving, the prosperity movement seeks to turn the relationship between God and individual people into a financial quid pro quo transaction. As scholar James R. Goff noted, God is "reduced to a kind of 'cosmic bellhop' attending to the needs and desires of his creation."[47] This is a wholly inadequate and unbiblical view of the relationship between God and people and the stewardship of wealth.

SUMMARY POINTS

- The prosperity gospel distorts the true gospel in that it does not point people toward Christ but rather focuses on the attainment of human desires.
- Prosperity gospel teachers misinterpret the Abrahamic covenant to be a promise of health and wealth for Christians who are obedient to God.

- Prosperity gospel advocates teach that the death of Christ results in financial and physical well-being for Christians.
- Common passages that are appealed to and misinterpreted in order to endorse the prosperity message are Ecclesiastes 11:1; Mark 10:30; 2 Corinthians 9:6; Galatians 6:7; and 3 John 2.
- A foundational reason why the prosperity gospel is off base is its faulty view of the relationship between God and people.

PART 2

CORRECTION

Chapter 4

The Biblical Teaching on Suffering

While followers of the prosperity gospel do not always explicitly state it, a main attraction of prosperity theology is its message concerning the avoidance or alleviation of suffering. Given that all people have an instinctive desire to escape suffering, this appeal is quite natural. Suffering takes different forms, yet, generally speaking, it falls into one of two broad, intertwined categories: physical suffering and mental (or emotional) suffering. Physical suffering includes any type of bodily harm or illness up to the point of death. Mental suffering entails such things as loss, fear, and personal failure.

In their preaching and teaching, advocates of the prosperity gospel speak in positive terms, focusing largely upon economic prosperity. Stated in the language of suffering, this is primarily a message of avoiding mental suffering over finances; yet, themes related to overcoming other types of suffering are present in prosperity theology too. Examples include the promise of flourishing in personal relationships, experiencing occupational success, and even tales of miraculous physical healings. Whether physical or mental, it is clear that the prosperity gospel places great emphasis on the avoidance of personal suffering.

As previous chapters have demonstrated, many tenets of the prosperity gospel are problematic at best and false at worst. The prosperity movement's doctrine of suffering is no exception, but it invites the question, "What does the Bible teach about suffering?" This is an important inquiry, for despite the questionable teaching on this topic by proponents of the prosperity gospel, suffering is part of human life and is experienced in varying degrees and in many different forms. Suffering is so common that oftentimes questions related to suffering are based as much on personal experience as they are upon intellectual curiosity. This seems true both of characters in the pages of Scripture and in contemporary life. In this age of instant mass communication where the knowledge of others' suffering becomes more widespread, inquiries related to the biblical perspective on suffering abound.

Although this chapter cannot provide a comprehensive answer to all the complex questions about pain and suffering, it will examine the biblical teaching on suffering, particularly with respect to the promises of the prosperity gospel about personal flourishing, both financially and otherwise. In this chapter we will survey a selection of biblical characters and teachings on suffering, briefly discuss some of the foundational causes of personal suffering, and suggest practical guidelines for believers to consider as they either experience or witness suffering in the world.

BIBLICAL CHARACTERS AND TEACHINGS

Pain and suffering are common among biblical characters. Old Testament examples are plentiful:

- Abraham spent his later years as a nomad in a foreign land. God declared that his firstborn son would be "a wild donkey of a man, his hand against everyone" (Gen. 16:12; see Gen. 21:9–12), and Abraham's life pilgrimage included marital and political strife.
- Jacob experienced pronounced dysfunction within his family, the rape of his daughter, and health challenges that included diminished eyesight and a crippled hip.
- Joseph was unjustly treated by his own brothers and spent years in prison for a crime he did not commit.

- Job lost everything he held dear—except for his wife and his life—including his children, possessions, and health.
- David endured ridicule from his family, persecution from his enemies, public humiliation, and the loss of more than one of his children.
- Many of the prophets—including Isaiah, Jeremiah, Ezekiel, and Daniel—endured rejection, slander, persecution, and even exile.

And there are many others.

New Testament examples of those who suffered are no less common. They include the crucified Christ—the Man of Sorrows—who was "mocked and shamefully treated and spit upon" (Luke 18:32); the twelve apostles, all of whom were persecuted and, according to church tradition, most of whom lost their lives for the sake of the gospel; and the apostle Paul, whose life was marked by suffering that included beatings on account of his faith, unjust prison sentences, death threats, shipwrecks, sleeplessness, hunger, and thirst (see 2 Cor. 11:22–29). Beyond the named personalities in the New Testament, it is evident from the narrative in the book of Acts, as well as the historical record in the Epistles, that pain and suffering were common among the early followers of Christ. It is difficult, if not impossible, to find anyone in either the Old or New Testament who experienced a pain-free life on account of their faith.

Explicit teachings concerning what believers can expect in regard to suffering include many biblical passages that all presume suffering to be a regular part of the Christian life. Paul writes to the Philippians, "For it has been granted to you that for the sake of Christ you should not only believe in him but also suffer for his sake" (Phil. 1:29). Likewise, Paul teaches his protégé, Timothy, "Indeed, all who desire to live a godly life in Christ Jesus will be persecuted" (2 Tim. 3:12). Peter informs the early church, "For to this you have been called, because Christ also suffered for you, leaving you an example, so that you might follow in his steps. . . . Therefore let those who suffer according to God's will entrust their souls to a faithful Creator" (1 Peter 2:21; 4:19). Scripture shows that faith in Christ is not a means to escape a life of suffering; rather, faith is often a reason for personal suffering.

Given that Jesus suffered greatly during His incarnation, it is reasonable to conclude that Christlikeness—which is the goal of the Christian life—will entail a degree of suffering.

Considering the subject theologically, one can likewise conclude that pain and suffering are a normative part of the Christian life. Given that Jesus suffered greatly during His incarnation, it is reasonable to conclude that Christlikeness—which is the goal of the Christian life—will entail a degree of suffering. This is the message Jesus Himself communicated to His followers, "If the world hates you, know that it has hated me before it hated you. . . . Remember the word that I said to you: 'A servant is not greater than his master.' If they persecuted me, they will also persecute you" (John 15:18, 20). Much of the New Testament terminology used to describe the Christian life is pregnant with overtones of experiencing suffering, including taking up one's cross (see Luke 9:23), being crucified with Christ (see Gal. 2:20), becoming a slave (see 1 Cor. 7:23), dying to self (see Rom. 6:6), being last in order to be first (see Matt. 20:16), becoming weak in order to be strong (see 2 Cor. 12:10), being poor in order to receive eternal riches (see Luke 6:20), losing one's life in order to save it (see Mark 8:35), and decreasing that the Lord might increase (see John 3:30). Both the examples and the explicit teachings of Scripture present suffering as a regular part of the Christian life.

CAUSES OF SUFFERING

Demonstrating that suffering is a normative part of the biblical record and everyday life is not a challenging task. A more demanding assignment is investigating the potential causes of such suffering. To frame this difficult issue, it will be helpful to analyze suffering (both physical and mental) under two broad headings: suffering caused by natural evil and suffering that stems from moral evil. Certainly natural evil and moral evil are related, frequently intertwined categories. Yet since the suffering that results from each type of evil, along with the rationale behind such suffering, is not always identical, it is beneficial to use these categories.

Suffering and Natural Evil

Simply defined, natural evil consists of things such as natural disasters (earthquakes, tornados, tsunamis, floods, droughts, and other "acts of God"), diseases, genetic defects, injuries, and death. Natural evil is not directly caused by the actions of another human being. This type of evil is a part of the fallen created order and, as such, involves material forces beyond human control. It is certain that within the biblical record, as well as in the present world, much suffering is caused by natural evil.

When a tornado strikes and takes a life, or when someone is diagnosed with a malignant cancer, the fallen human mind almost defaults to thoughts of divine judgment. In a manner reminiscent of Job's friends, natural evil and its resultant suffering are often assumed to be directly tied to the morality of those who are affected by it. While the account of Job makes it clear that such a conclusion is not necessarily warranted, it is true that the biblical narrative includes examples of divinely initiated suffering through natural (or even supernatural) evil on account of moral corruption. For instance, in Noah's day God caused a great flood when He "saw that the wickedness of man was great in the earth, and that every intention of the thoughts of his heart was only evil continually. . . . So the Lord said, 'I will blot out man whom I have created from the face of the land, man and animals and creeping things and birds of the heavens, for I am sorry that I have made them'" (Gen. 6:5, 7). Likewise, in the account of the annihilation of Sodom and Gomorrah, Lot's angelic visitors testified, "We are about to destroy this place, because the outcry against its people has become great before the LORD, and the LORD has sent us to destroy it. . . . Then the LORD rained on Sodom and Gomorrah sulfur and fire from the LORD out of heaven" (Gen. 19:13, 24). In spite of these examples where God judged sin by allowing suffering through natural evil, this is not the normative biblical pattern. Such examples are exceptions, not the rule.

To get a comprehensive picture of the place of natural evil in the present world, one must go back to the creation narrative in the book of Genesis. Genesis 1–2 reports that the Lord made the world good. In fact, the teaching that the creation was "good" is a mantra that beats throughout the first two chapters of Scripture (see Gen. 1:4, 10, 12, 18, 21, 25, 31; 2:9, 12). Natural evil and suffering were not part of God's original design—that is, they were not part of God's good created order. As Genesis 3 reports, however, soon after creation humankind rebelled against the Lord, pridefully desiring to be like God Himself. As a result of this rebellion, natural evil entered the created order. The apostle Paul, reflecting on the fall, writes, "Sin came into the world through one man, and death through sin, and so death spread to all men because all sinned" (Rom. 5:12). This is what the Lord had graciously warned about in Genesis 2:16–17 with His admonition, "You may surely eat of every tree of the garden, but of the tree of the knowledge of good and evil you shall not eat, for in the day that you eat of it you shall surely die." It was on account of the sin of humanity that God cursed the created order, and suffering due to natural evil became a reality.

Natural evil and suffering were not part of God's original design.

While the narrative of Genesis 1–3 explains *how* suffering through natural evil entered the created order, it does not clearly address the question of *why* the Lord allowed such suffering to become a possibility. Although the greater concern here is the causes of suffering (i.e., the "how" of suffering) rather than the reasons for suffering (i.e., the "why" of suffering), a brief word concerning the rationale for suffering via natural evil is in order.

A survey of the Gospels reveals two instances in which Jesus addressed the "why" of personal suffering that stems from natural evil.

On one occasion Jesus refers to "those eighteen on whom the tower in Siloam fell and killed them: do you think that they were worse offenders than all the others who lived in Jerusalem? No, I tell you; but unless you repent, you will all likewise perish" (Luke 13:4–5). John records the second occasion, "As he [Jesus] passed by, he saw a man blind from birth. And his disciples asked him, 'Rabbi, who sinned, this man or his parents, that he was born blind?' Jesus answered, 'It was not that this man sinned, or his parents, but that the works of God might be displayed in him'" (John 9:1–3). According to Jesus, while suffering may not be directly caused by personal sin, suffering on account of natural evil occurs as a reminder of the need to repent of one's own sinful condition, as well as to provide an opportunity for God's works to be displayed.[1]

Much personal suffering is the result of natural evil, and the possibility of such suffering stems from God's curse on the created order at the fall of humankind. Even so, as the biblical narrative unfolds, it becomes clear that the purpose of such suffering is ultimately to foster a person's relationship with the Lord. The present curse on creation, along with the resultant suffering, is a manifestation of God's grace, not His wrath. Perhaps this is how Paul, reflecting on Genesis 3:14–19, could write, "For the creation was subjected to futility, not willingly, but because of him who subjected it, *in hope*" (Rom. 8:20, emphasis added). Ethicist John Frame aptly captures this teaching as he writes, "Scripture, therefore, gives us an explicit answer to the problem of natural evil. Natural evil is a curse brought upon the world because of moral evil. It functions as punishment to the wicked and as a means of discipline for those who are righteous by God's grace. It also reminds us of the cosmic dimensions of sin and redemption."[2]

Suffering and Moral Evil

In contrast to natural evil, which is largely impersonal and is usually manifest as a defect in the created order, moral evil is always personal and finds its genesis in the human heart. To engage in moral evil is to willfully break the law of God. Given the apostle John's teaching that "sin is lawlessness" (1 John 3:4), moral evil can be simply defined as sin.

In other words, moral evil is to fall short of the law of God, which is the standard by which He judges the world. Both life experience and Scripture testify that there is an inherent connection between moral evil and personal suffering. Regarding this link Paul writes, "Whatever one sows, that will he also reap. For the one who sows to his own flesh will from the flesh reap corruption" (Gal. 6:7–8). In daily living this "corruption" is experienced as suffering on account of personal sin, as well as suffering that stems from being caught in the sin of another.

Interestingly, the teaching that personal, moral evil engenders suffering is not a stumbling block for most people, whether they are believers or not. In his first letter to the church, Peter writes rather matter-of-factly about "suffer[ing] for . . . doing evil" (3:17) and of "suffer[ing] as a murderer or a thief or an evildoer or as a meddler" (4:15). The apostle did not feel compelled to justify this teaching, nor is it often questioned today. Perhaps this phenomenon can be explained: In light of the fact that the moral law is a reflection of God's character, and given that people are made in God's image, most people do not question the justice of suffering on account of their own lawlessness. It seems quite logical that individuals should suffer for their own expressions of moral evil such as folly, bad judgment, self-righteousness, immaturity, pride, and a host of other sins. In fact, the penalties, which are a form of suffering themselves, tied to modern civil laws rest on the general acceptance of this.

Suffering on account of the moral evil of another, however, frequently raises questions of justice. When a bystander suffers because of another's rage, drunken driving, stealing, rape, or even simple negligence, it is natural to question the equity of such events. Scripture does, however, contain insight into secondary suffering. The prophet Ezekiel declares, "The son shall not suffer for the iniquity of the father, nor the father suffer for the iniquity of the son" (Ezek. 18:20). Yet, the Bible also makes mention of suffering due to the sin of another when it describes the Lord "visiting the iniquity of the fathers on the children, to the third and the fourth generation" (Num. 14:18; see Exod. 20:5; 34:7). These seemingly contradictory biblical teachings can be reconciled by understanding the distinction between being affected by the sin of another and being judged for the sin of another. While God holds individuals accountable for their own sins, given the integrated nature of the fallen world, individual sin always has a corporate effect. While this may not seem just, it is a part of communal life in the fallen world.

Three main sources of suffering exist in this present world: the curse on the created order, personal sin, and the sins of others. Suffering the effect of the curse on the world is to suffer under natural evil. Suffering that stems from individual sin, whether one's own or that of another, is to suffer the effects of moral evil. While it is never pleasant, most people do not usually question suffering that stems from personal sin. It is suffering on account of another's sin, as well as suffering because of the curse on the created order that often raises questions about divine justice. Jesus teaches that the purpose of such suffering is to remind one of personal sin and the need for repentance, as well as to provide an opportunity for God's works to be displayed.

CONSIDERATIONS FOR SUFFERING

It is not the intent of this chapter to provide a comprehensive answer to all of the complex questions related to pain and suffering. Rather, we seek to give an overview of biblical teaching on suffering with the goal of both correcting the false doctrine of the prosperity gospel and providing scriptural guidance on this important topic. Some basic considerations follow for believers to review as they either experience or witness suffering in the present world. While these considerations are not intended to make pain and suffering more physically tolerable, emotionally easier, or even more intellectually satisfying, hopefully they will prove to be of spiritual benefit for those who grapple with questions related to personal suffering.

Everyone Is a Sinner

The creation narrative records the fact that God made the world good, indeed proclaiming all that He had made to be "very good" (Gen. 1:31). Thus, there was a time when pain and suffering did not exist. People freely chose, however, to rebel against God, and ushered sin and the possibility of suffering into the world (see Rom. 5:12). Many who raise questions about the justice of suffering overlook or minimize the fact that people were the conduit through which sin and suffering entered the world in the first place.

Oftentimes questions about the equity of suffering are formed with the presupposition of the moral goodness (or at least moral neutrality) of humans. This assumption leads to the claim that personal suffering is not just, for if people are essentially good, suffering is undeserved. However, Scripture not only records the role and culpability of people in allowing sin into the world but also testifies to their moral corruption. The prophet Isaiah declares that, when measured by the Lord's standards, "all our righteous deeds are like a polluted garment" (Isa. 64:6), and Paul reports God's conclusion that "none is righteous, no, not one . . . no one does good, not even one" (Rom. 3:10–12). When personal suffering is viewed in light of the sinful condition of humanity, it becomes evident that all people are disqualified from charging God with injustice. While a given instance of suffering may not be deserved (in the sense that it was not caused by one's own immediate sin), when compared to the eternal condemnation that all people ultimately deserve for their sin, charges of divine inequity quickly dissipate. Given the grace that the Lord affords sinful man in His mercy and long-suffering, such consideration ought to move one to praise God who "shows his love for us in that while we were still sinners, Christ died for us" (Rom. 5:8).

Everyone Possesses a Free Will

Another consideration that may be taken into account when discussing personal suffering is the fact that everyone possesses a free will. The idea and parameters of free will are topics that theologians have debated for centuries.[3] As the concept is commonly understood, at a minimum having a free will entails the ability to freely choose from among available options. While most would affirm that having a free will is a good thing, given the fallen state of humankind, the concept of a free will necessarily includes the ability to choose to sin. Such sinful choices often result in suffering, both on account of personal sin and due to the sins of others. Interestingly, though, few people question God's justice when they are in the midst of freely choosing to sin. No one charges God with inequity when they are not punished for cheating on their taxes, exceeding the speed limit, or freely gossiping about the happenings of church business meetings. Rather, people tend to accuse the Lord of being unjust when they personally suffer, or perhaps when they witness the suffering of others on a grand scale (natural disasters, terrorist attacks, warfare, etc.). Such an approach betrays the self-righteous, self-centered bent of many discussions over pain and suffering.

In light of the corrupt nature of all people, it becomes apparent that the only way for the Lord to prevent pain and suffering in the present world without altering human free will would be for Him to destroy people (since suffering is caused by their moral evil or the natural evil that stems from their original sin). Of course, another option was for God Himself to bear the penalty for human sin in the death of His Son, Jesus Christ. In so doing God truly experienced unjust suffering and affords people the opportunity to dwell forever on a restored earth where there will be no pain and suffering. Paul writes of this divine substitution and the prospect for imputed righteousness: "In Christ God was reconciling the world to himself, not counting their trespasses against them. . . . For our sake he made him to be sin who knew no sin, so that in him we might become the righteousness of God" (2 Cor. 5:19, 21).

There Is Value in Suffering

A comforting consideration for those who are in the midst of personal trials may be the fact that there is value in suffering—though the value is usually not seen until time has passed. While Paul's teaching that "all things work together for good" (Rom. 8:28) may sound trite to someone in the throes of personal loss, most would agree in retrospect that past seasons of suffering have been times of great personal growth. This does not mean, of course, that suffering is good. Suffering in itself is not good; yet, God has the ability to use suffering for good. The uncertainty that is part of the relationship between suffering and personal growth, as well as the perspective that is usually needed to appreciate this dynamic, ought to prevent one from developing a "martyr complex" on account of the potential value of suffering. These caveats notwithstanding, it is possible to identify several practical and spiritual benefits of suffering.

Suffering in itself is not good; yet, God has the ability to use suffering for good.

Perhaps the most obvious practical benefit of suffering is that it can be a warning sign of approaching danger. This is true in a physical sense, such as when pain is a sign that one's bodily limits have been reached, or when minor pain is a symptom of a more serious disease that can be treated. Likewise, as previously noted, suffering can be a practical reminder of one's need to repent. Jesus teaches this (see Luke 13:1–5), and the writer of Hebrews applies it to one's own personal suffering when he writes that suffering "seems painful rather than pleasant, but later it yields the peaceful fruit of righteousness to those who have been trained by it" (Heb. 12:11).

Another sometimes overlooked, practical benefit of suffering is that it can lead to relationships that would not otherwise be established—that is, it has the potential to result in what could be called a fellowship of suffering. While the phrase "misery loves company" is often used pejoratively, it remains true that trials afford sufferers the opportunity both to comfort and to minister to one another. The apostle Paul appeals to this truth as he writes to the Corinthian church, "If we are afflicted, it is for your comfort and salvation. . . . Our hope for you is unshaken, for we know that as you share in our sufferings, you will also share in our comfort" (2 Cor. 1:6–7).

One final practical benefit of suffering is that the gospel can be advanced when nonbelievers see Christians react in an appropriate way to trials. Paul refers to this as manifesting the life of Jesus in the flesh (see 2 Cor. 4:11), a process that the apostle himself demonstrated when unjustly incarcerated in Philippi (see Acts 16:25), as well as when under house arrest in Rome (see Phil. 1:12–14).

Arguably, though, the practical benefits of trials are eclipsed by the spiritual value of suffering. The greatest benefit of suffering is the sanctification it fosters by forcing people to rely upon God. When people flourish, there is little need for divine dependence. Conversely, when believers struggle, they rarely wander far from the Lord. When faced with his unidentified "thorn in the flesh," the apostle Paul prays three times for relief; yet, each time Jesus' response is, "My grace is sufficient for you, for my power is made perfect in weakness" (2 Cor. 12:9). This dynamic is behind the proverb, "Give me neither poverty nor riches; feed me with the food that is needful for me, lest I be full and deny you and say, 'Who is the Lord?' or lest I be poor and steal and profane the name of my God" (Prov. 30:8–9). Trials also allow people to identify with Christ. The trials of life, especially unjust pain and suffering, can give people a glimpse of Jesus' experience on the cross. Such Christlike suffering can teach obedience (see Heb. 5:8), confirm salvation (see Rom. 8:17), and ultimately provide eternal reward (see Acts 14:22).

God Is Acquainted with Suffering

An important consideration in the midst of pain and suffering is that God Himself is acquainted with suffering. Christianity is unique in its doctrine of the incarnation of Christ—that is, the teaching that God Himself took on flesh and voluntarily became part of the fellowship of human suffering. Jesus Christ was not just peripherally acquainted with suffering; He experienced intense physical and spiritual suffering—all on account of His display of perfect love. In fact, given Jesus' sinless life, He is the only person in all of history who truly suffered unjustly. Consider some of the passages that describe the intense personal suffering of Christ: "[Jesus] said to them, 'My soul is very sorrowful, even to death'" (Mark 14:34); "And being in an agony he prayed more earnestly; and his sweat became like great drops of blood falling down to the ground" (Luke 22:44); and, in one of the most arresting statements in all of Scripture, "About the ninth hour Jesus cried out with a loud voice, saying . . . 'My God, my God, why have you forsaken me?'" (Matt. 27:46). These passages are even more meaningful in light of the fact that Jesus was aware of His impending suffering long before it occurred, even teaching His disciples about it (see Matt. 16:21; Luke 9:22), yet He willingly accepted it on behalf of humanity (see Isa. 53:7; Heb. 2:10; 5:8).

For believers who are suffering, the fact that the fellowship of suffering includes Christ ought to be comforting. As the writer of Hebrews notes, "Since therefore the children share in flesh and blood, he himself likewise partook of the same things. . . . For because he himself has suffered when tempted, he is able to help those who are being tempted" (Heb. 2:14, 18). The encouragement that comes from Jesus' suffering should not be limited to believers' identification with Him or even to His example for His followers. Rather, the reason for Christ's suffering must be kept in mind—that is, He suffered as a substitute, receiving the just penalty for the sins of humankind. As Isaiah prophesied, "He has borne our griefs and carried our sorrows. . . . He was wounded for our transgressions; he was crushed for our iniquities; upon him was the chastisement that brought us peace, and with his stripes we are healed" (Isa. 53:4–5). This teaching is important, for it means that while Christians may be disciplined out of God's love (see Heb. 12:3–11), they are not afflicted out of God's wrath. While pain and suffering will abound in the fallen world, the reason for believers' suffering cannot be divine retribution for sins, for Jesus already suffered and died for the sins of His followers. The price has been paid. In the words of Christ, "It is finished" (John 19:30).

For believers who are suffering, the fact that the fellowship of suffering includes Christ ought to be comforting.

God Is Sovereign

One final consideration that may be taken into account in the midst of pain and suffering is the fact that God is sovereign over all things. God's sovereignty includes both what He does, as well as His allowance of events that He knows will happen. No trials occur apart from God's sovereign purview. While some have tried to use the presence of suffering in the world to argue against God's sovereignty or His goodness (or both), the witness of Scripture is that the Lord is sovereign enough to use suffering in order to accomplish His plans, as well as good enough to allow His children to experience the trials needed to conform them to His image. The apostle Paul puts it this way, "For this light momentary affliction is preparing for us an eternal weight of glory beyond all comparison. . . . I consider that the sufferings of this present time are not worth comparing with the glory that is to be revealed to us" (2 Cor. 4:17; Rom. 8:18). Reflecting on Jesus' teachings and example of suffering, New Testament scholar Dan McCartney notes, "Suffering truly is necessary; it is not arbitrary or haphazard but purposeful. Therefore, while the proximate cause of suffering may be evil, its presence in the overall scheme of things is for biblical writers not something that calls God's goodness into question; rather, it is the means by which God's goodness is expressed."[4]

In spite of the fact that in His sovereignty God uses suffering to bring about good, one must not confuse this with the idea that suffering is good. There is a great difference between the teaching that God is sovereign enough to use suffering in the fallen world in order to bring about good, and the idea that God desires or needs suffering in order to accomplish good. Perhaps the clearest picture of this is the reaction of Jesus at the death of His friend Lazarus. In his gospel, John reports that even though Jesus was about to raise Lazarus from the dead—an event of which Jesus was certainly aware—He still openly wept upon arriving at the tomb of Lazarus. Christ had already taught His disciples that Lazarus's death was not permanent but was "for the glory of God, so that the Son of God may be glorified through it" (John 11:4), yet He nevertheless shed tears when faced with the ravages of natural evil. Thus, while suffering affords the Lord an opportunity to be glorified (see Rom. 11:32; James 5:11), and He is certainly sovereign enough to do so, the truth that sin and suffering grieve the heart of God ought not to be overlooked. The Lord does not need suffering in order to be good; rather, in His sovereignty God is able to use suffering for good.

CONCLUSION

Scripture presents suffering as a normative part of the Christian life. Contrary to the claims of some advocates of the prosperity gospel, suffering is not an indicator of lack of faith; rather, suffering and persecutions are likely to increase with faith. While the Bible does not present suffering as desirable, it likewise does not view suffering as a hindrance to God's plan of redemption. While a day is coming in the future in which there will be no more pain and suffering, Scripture teaches that in the current fallen world trials are a tool that the Lord uses in order to foster the sanctification of His people.

SUMMARY POINTS

- The prosperity gospel focuses upon the avoidance of suffering, including financial, mental, and physical suffering.
- Pain and suffering are common among biblical characters, including David, Jesus, and Paul.
- Suffering is a normative part of the Christian life and, this side of the grave, is likely to increase with maturing faith.
- Three main sources of suffering exist in this present world: the curse on the created order, personal sin, and the sins of others.
- Considerations for suffering include the following facts: everyone is a sinner, everyone possesses a free will, there is value in suffering, God is acquainted with suffering, and God is sovereign.

Chapter 5

The Biblical Teaching on Wealth and Poverty

An aspect of the prosperity gospel that makes it attractive to many believers is that it contains elements of biblical truth. Historically speaking, this has been a mark of nearly all false teaching and heresy; few would accept teaching that was clearly unbiblical.[1] Within evangelical circles, the degree to which the prosperity gospel has retained elements of biblical truth is generally the degree to which it has been adopted by Bible-believing Christians. Especially egregious examples of prosperity theology, such as the teachings of those who are more openly associated with the New Thought movement, have not been as accepted as the ideas of soft advocates of the prosperity gospel such as Joel Osteen, Joyce Meyer, and T. D. Jakes. Yet, the degree to which truth and error is mixed in a given doctrine ought not to be viewed as a barometer of authenticity; for in regard to absolute truth, a teaching that is only partially true is completely false. In the church, so-called "half-truths" are often more dangerous than overt lies, for their potential to deceive is far greater.

Certainly the mixture of truth and error in the teachings of the prosperity gospel often makes it difficult to separate fact from fiction; yet, a more foundational issue is the question of why so many contemporary Christians adopt prosperity theology in the first place. The inescapable conclusion is that many believers do not have a firm grasp on what the Bible actually teaches in regard to wealth and poverty. While there are surely many reasons for this lack of knowledge, three stand out. First, many Christians do not view wealth and poverty as topics for moral discussion. While many have a general idea that the gospel should prompt them to give to the church and perhaps even exhibit care for the poor, the bigger picture issues—such as how material wealth/poverty and spiritual wealth/poverty relate (if at all)—are more removed from their minds. Consequently, if one is not even aware that Scripture contains a specific ethic of wealth and poverty—let alone what that ethic entails—little knowledge will be available to draw upon when confronted with false teaching related to finances.

The best defense against the teachings of the prosperity gospel is a holistic understanding of scriptural teaching on wealth and poverty.

A second reason for the lack of knowledge on issues related to wealth and poverty is the scarcity of biblical teaching on the subject within the church. For example, the Christian Stewardship Association reports that only 10 percent of churches actively teach biblical stewardship and less than 4 percent of Christian colleges and seminaries offer courses on the use of money.[2] It is no wonder that so many believers are susceptible to the teaching of the prosperity gospel. The lack of teaching on finances is compounded by the fact that often material that is presented in the church is theologically skewed either toward traditionally moderate emphases such as mercy ministries, or toward more conservative ideas such as investing and budgeting. While all aspects of biblical teaching on wealth and poverty are important, overemphasizing any one particular area at the expense of another risks distorting the entire doctrine. The best defense against the teachings of the prosperity gospel is a holistic understanding of scriptural teaching on wealth and poverty.

A third reason for ignorance in the church over wealth and poverty-related issues is the fact that the biblical material seems contradictory or inconsistent in places. For example, at one end of the economic spectrum, Scripture appears to present poverty as both a blessing and a curse. Compare Proverbs 23:21, which warns, "The drunkard and the glutton will come to poverty," with Jesus' teaching in Luke 6:20, which reads, "Blessed are you who are poor, for yours is the kingdom of God."[3] Likewise, at the other end of the economic spectrum, a number of passages describe wealth as both a blessing and a curse. Moses taught Israel, "It is [the Lord your God] who gives you power to get wealth" (Deut. 8:18); yet Jesus observed in Matthew 19:23, "Only with difficulty will a rich person enter the kingdom of heaven." The biblical narrative is replete with examples of wealthy and poor individuals, who are either godly or ungodly, but not along consistent lines or according to a regular pattern. Such paradoxical examples can confuse readers and discourage believers from attempting to construct a coherent biblical ethic of wealth and poverty.

In light of these issues, we will explore the biblical teaching on wealth and poverty in hopes of shedding light on the topic and providing believers with a defense against the false teachings of the prosperity gospel.

THE BOOK OF GENESIS

A logical starting place for investigating the biblical teaching on wealth and poverty is the book of Genesis. In fact, it is only within the first two chapters of Genesis that one can find material related to this topic, or any topic for that matter, in a perfect, sinless, pre-fallen setting. The creation narrative is important for the topic of wealth and poverty because it yields a significant piece of information; namely, God created humankind with material needs.[4] These included the need for food (see Gen. 1:29; 2:9, 16), water (see Gen. 2:6, 10–14), companionship (see Gen. 2:18), rest (see Gen. 2:1–4; Mark 2:27), as well as a presumably temperate climate and adequate shelter. This observation means that the presence of material needs in the world, as well as the desire to meet them, cannot be inherently sinful. Therefore, while some tend to imagine perfection or paradise (or perhaps envision heaven) to be a state without material needs, this conclusion does not seem to be warranted by the text.[5] Rather, for pre-fallen humans, paradise consisted of a divinely designed state in which men and women had the ability to meet their material needs.

The creation narrative reveals that not only were people created by God with material needs, but they also were placed by the Lord in an environment that was capable of meeting those needs—the same environment in which they dwell today, albeit now in a sin-tainted, fallen state. In other words, as image-bearers of God, people were set in an ideal world and assigned with working in order to satisfy their material needs.[6] Before sin entered the created order, humans were both laborers, charged with ruling and filling the earth (see Gen. 1:26, 28), and consumers, being given herbs and trees for food (see Gen. 1:29; 2:9).[7] Presumably, if they were successful in their labors, they had the ability to satisfy their material needs and perhaps even to generate wealth. Conversely, had they neglected their material needs, it would have resulted in poverty, or at least in a continued state of want.

While Adam was immediately faithful in his stewardship of the created order, dutifully naming the animals (see Gen. 2:19–20), speculation about what would have happened over time if he had either continued or neglected to work becomes a moot point, for Scripture indicates that the tenure of the man and his wife in the garden of Eden was apparently short-lived.[8] Immediately following the creation narrative of Genesis 1–2, the text records the fall of humankind in Genesis 3, an event that forever altered the lives of the first couple, along with the lives of those who would follow. While the fall of humanity was primarily a spiritual event, involving people's attempt to usurp God's authority, thereby worshiping themselves rather than their Creator, there were material aspects to the fall as well. However the fall did not create humanity's material needs, nor does Scripture indicate that it increased them. The fall and ensuing curse significantly affected the environment in which people labor, as well as their desire to work in order to satisfy their own material needs.

As a part of the curse at the fall, the creation narrative records that the woman would no longer be a willing helper to her husband, the work for which she was created (see Gen. 2:18), nor would she find childbirth to be without pain (see Gen. 3:16). Likewise, the man would no longer be able to work the ground with ease in order to provide for and to protect his family, for the earth would now produce thorns and thistles, turning labor into toil (see Gen. 3:17–19). Yet, despite the curse that the created order was put under and the hardships that it entailed, the man and woman's duty to fulfill their material needs remained intact. Although they were placed under a curse for their sin, constitutionally speaking, they were (and still are) image-bearers of God—the fall did not alter this fact (see Gen. 9:5–6; 1 Cor. 11:7). Given that labor is one of the ways in which humankind functionally bears the image of God, the responsibility to work in order to satisfy material needs persists.[9] This condition and duty are components of creational design.

Although it was touched upon in the preceding chapter, it may be helpful to note why the Lord placed the created order under a curse and made it more difficult for people to satisfy their material needs—inevitably increasing the potential for poverty. In his epistle to the Romans, Paul addresses this issue as he explains, "For the creation waits with eager longing for the revealing of the sons of God. For the creation was subjected to futility, not willingly, but because of him who subjected it, in hope" (Rom. 8:19–20; see Gen. 3:17). It was not out of anger that God cursed the ground, nor was it an attempt to create material hardships for men and women as retributive punishment. Rather, the Lord subjected the created order to the effects of sin out of love, in hope that it would drive people back to the Lord from whom they had fled, with the realization that God is the Creator, Sustainer, and Provider of all things. Not surprisingly, as both Jesus' teaching and life experience testify, it is the poor—those who most acutely feel the material effects of the fall—who come to Christ in the greatest numbers (see Matt. 5:3; Luke 6:20).[10]

THE OLD TESTAMENT LAW

The Old Testament law is a body of legislation recorded in the Pentateuch—the first five books of the Bible—that contains hundreds of regulations, given for the purpose of ordering the Hebrew theocracy (a God-centered model of government). While the context of Scripture reveals that certain laws are only directly applicable to theocratic Israel—it is nonetheless widely recognized that these laws are time-bound cultural applications of unchanging moral principles.[11] A review of the economic portions of the Old Testament law can help contemporary readers understand the timeless moral framework upon which the biblical teaching on wealth and poverty rests.

Dozens of regulations in the law address the economic life of God's people and most of them relate to the institution of the Sabbath, which had three different manifestations within the Hebrew theocracy. First, there was the Sabbath Day, which many believers recognize as the fourth commandment, although it is articulated apart from the Ten Commandments as well (see Exod. 20:8–11; 23:12; Lev. 23:3; Deut. 5:12–15). The Sabbath Day prescribed the cessation of ordinary labors, for both people and animals, one out of every seven days. Second, there was the Sabbath Year, which was to be observed every seventh year (see Exod. 23:10–11; Lev. 25:1–7; Deut. 15:1–18).[12] During the Sabbath Year, people, animals, and the land were to rest from their regular work. Additionally, all outstanding debts between Jews were to be cancelled. Third, the institution of the Sabbath was manifest in the Year of Jubilee (see Lev. 25:8–55; 27:16–25). The Jubilee, which was to be celebrated every fiftieth year—after seven cycles of the Sabbath Year—involved the rest of people, animals, and the ground, as well as the return of all lands and most houses to their original owners.[13]

Although economic aspects of the law address a variety of issues, ranging from rest and labor to usury and philanthropy, all of the legislation related to wealth and poverty seems to be oriented toward achieving the same two goals. The first of these goals is promoting the creation ideal of laboring and resting (i.e., trusting) in the Lord in order to meet material needs. While the fall resulted in a curse on the ground and on humanity, it did not diminish the pre-fall responsibility of people to labor in order to meet material needs. The Sabbath structure that underpinned many of the wealth and poverty-related regulations within the law helped order Jewish social life by encouraging a schedule of labor and rest, which included formal worship and even leisure time.[14] By observing this regular cycle of labor and rest, and in keeping the related economic laws, the Jews were able to functionally bear God's image and testify to the goodness of creational design. The pattern of labor and rest communicated by the economic laws fostered trust in the Lord by preventing God's people from making work an ultimate source of security, and it demonstrated God's plan of redemption, which comes by resting in the Lord and not by works (see Isa. 56:4–7; Ezek. 20:12).

A second goal toward which the economic aspects of the law seem to be oriented is protection of the people from sins related to wealth and poverty. Although it is true that the underlying Sabbath structure of the economic regulations benefited everyone by offering rest and thereby helping to mitigate the effects of the fall (see Gen. 3:19), a more specific focus of these laws is preventing oppression of the poor by the sins of the rich. For example, the aim of protecting the poor can be seen in the following civil laws: cancellation of debts on the Sabbath Year (see Deut. 15:1–3), a ban on prorating benevolence in view of the approaching Sabbath Year (see Deut. 15:9–10), the reversion of property in the Year of Jubilee (see Lev. 25:8–34), the freeing of indentured servants in the Year of Jubilee (see Lev. 25:35–55),[15] and the continuation of gleaning rights during the Sabbath Year (see Exod. 23:11), among many other economic regulations. In short, laws such as these recognized the potential for oppression of the poor by the rich and sought to orient Hebrew society toward the ideal of provision for all.[16]

Yet, it should be noted that the economic laws of the Hebrew theocracy did not prevent or even discourage one from accumulating wealth—or, for that matter, from becoming poor. The possession or lack of material goods is not commended or condemned anywhere in Scripture, *per se*. Rather, the Bible condemns sins that either contribute to or stem from wealth and poverty. The ideal that the Old Testament economic laws were designed to protect was not equality but justice. Not only were people freely allowed to become wealthy or poor within each Sabbath cycle, but everything was not economically reset by the various manifestations of the Sabbath. For example, the law allowed for houses within walled towns to be sold permanently (see Lev. 25:29–30),[17] as well as for voluntarily lifelong joining of a servant to a beloved master (see Deut.

15:12–18). These laws highlight the fact that while justice does uphold the ideal of provision for all, it does not require an egalitarian distribution of resources. As ethicist John Frame has noted, equality is not mandated in Scripture, for economic prosperity (or the lack thereof) is not a zero-sum balance equation.[18] In view of justice and in recognition of the reality of sin, the economic portions of the Old Testament law were designed to protect and to correct distortions in the paradigm of labor being a means to meet material needs.

**The possession or lack of material goods
is not commended or condemned
anywhere in Scripture, *per se.***

THE PROPHETS AND THE WRITINGS

As the Jewish nation grew and moved from a theocratic form of government to a monarchical form of government, the people faced a number of new economic challenges. These included Israelite kings avoiding the self-exaltation that can come with the accumulation of excess wealth (see Deut. 17:16–17), issues related to governmental taxation (see 1 Sam. 8:10–18),[19] and the continued duty to tithe (see Mal. 3:8–12; the concept of tithing will be addressed in chapter 6). Yet, the foundations of biblical teaching on wealth and poverty remained the same—that is, continued endorsement of the goodness of laboring in order to meet material needs, as well as the duty to protect the poor from being oppressed by the rich. The economic material in the Old Testament that comes after the Law can be summarized as follows: the historical books narrate the Jews' (especially their kings') record of wealth and poverty; the Wisdom Literature upholds and espouses creational economic ideals; and the prophetic books confront the Jews for their failure to deal appropriately with wealth and poverty.

Within the Prophets and Writings—the books of the Old Testament that follow the Pentateuch—the wisdom books likely contain the greatest amount of material related to economics. The creation ideal of laboring in order to meet material needs is frequently mentioned in Wisdom Literature. For example, the book of Proverbs reports that "the hand of the diligent makes [one] rich. . . . Whoever works his land will have plenty of bread" (Prov. 10:4; 28:19).[20] Likewise, labor is implicitly encouraged in the wisdom books by warnings against idleness such as, "A little sleep, a little slumber, a little folding of the hands to rest, and poverty will come upon you like a robber, and want like an armed man. . . . An idle person will suffer hunger. . . . Love not sleep, lest you come to poverty" (Prov. 6:10–11; 19:15; 20:13).[21] The ideal of labor being productive is also upheld by warnings against mortgaging one's future against the unnecessary incurrence of debt (see Prov. 22:7) and by repeated discouragement of practices such as becoming surety for the loans of another (see Prov. 6:1–5; 11:15; 17:18; 20:16; 22:26; 27:13).

The duty to protect and care for the poor is also frequently prescribed in the Wisdom Literature. The book of Proverbs encourages believers, "Open your mouth, judge righteously, defend the rights of the poor and needy" (Prov. 31:9). Readers are also warned against oppressing the poor through usurious loans and extortion (see Ps. 15:5; Prov. 28:8; Ezek. 18:8, 13). The wisdom books also explicitly link righteousness with generosity (see Prov. 14:21; 29:7; 31:20), even equating lending to the poor with lending to the Lord (see Prov. 17:5; 19:17), a theme that appears in the New Testament as well (see Matt. 25:31–46). Conversely, other passages warn of divine retribution for ignoring the poor. For instance, Proverbs 21:13 states, "Whoever closes his ear to the cry of the poor will himself call out and not be answered." The theme of the Lord delivering the poor from the oppression of the wicked is so prevalent in the Psalms that theologian John Stott concludes, "The Psalter is the hymnbook of the helpless."[22] Passages such as these, which reiterate the foundational wealth and poverty related emphases first detailed in the creation narrative and law are scattered throughout the remainder of the Old Testament.

THE GOSPELS

All of the Old Testament laws relating to wealth and poverty were in effect for Israel in New Testament times, yet in all probability, not all were kept. This is true not only because of the moral and spiritual decline of God's people but also because Israel was under Roman rule and taxation from at least 63 B.C. throughout the New Testament era. This foreign occupation led to the impoverishment of many and made observance of the full body of Old Testament economic laws and principles difficult, if not impossible. This was the world into which Jesus Christ was born. Jesus' life and teachings each have something to contribute to a biblical ethic of wealth and poverty.

During His earthly ministry, Jesus attended to and identified with many from the lower classes, and Jesus frequently interacted with the religious elite.

Establishing a detailed ethic of wealth and poverty from the example of Christ's life can be challenging, for it is possible to emphasize both wealth and poverty in Jesus' life and ministry. Focusing on poverty, one could accentuate the fact that Jesus was born in a manger (see Luke 2:7) and that He was part of a lower or, at best, middle-class working family. Jesus' earthly father, Joseph, was a manual laborer—a carpenter (see Matt. 13:55), a trade that Christ Himself apparently later adopted (see Mark 6:3). At Jesus' birth Joseph and Mary were poor enough to qualify to offer two pigeons at the birth purification ceremony, rather than the usual yearling lamb (see Luke 2:24).[23] During His earthly ministry, Jesus attended to and identified with many from the lower classes—including prostitutes, orphans, widows, and other social and economic outcasts—even declaring, "Foxes have holes, and birds of the air have nests, but the Son of Man has nowhere to lay his head" (Matt. 8:20). This was true of Christ's life, as during His ministry He apparently had no home, no land, and no regular income.[24] Borrowing was a common practice during Jesus' earthly ministry—He borrowed a boat from which to preach, food to multiply, a colt on which to ride, a room in which to meet, and even a tomb in which to be buried.[25]

Conversely, though, the Gospels demonstrate power and material wealth in Jesus' life and ministry. Jesus frequently interacted with the religious elite, such as the scribes, Sadducees, and Pharisees, as well as members of the Sanhedrin, including Nicodemus and Joseph of Arimathea (see John 3:1–21; 19:38). Christ also ministered to powerful and wealthy individuals like the rich young ruler (see Matt. 19:16–24), the unnamed centurion (see Luke 7:1–5), and a number of tax collectors, including Levi and Zacchaeus.[26] Jesus occasionally attended public parties and feasts (see Luke 5:29–32; John 2:1–11), accepted invitations to dine with the rich and powerful (see Luke 11:37; 14:1–6), used investment banking analogies in order to illustrate His parables (see Matt. 25:14–30; Luke 19:11–27), and on more than one occasion, graciously received costly gifts from His followers (see Luke 7:36–39; John 12:1–3). By Jesus' own testimony, "The Son of Man came eating and drinking" (Matt. 11:19). Moreover, while the verse has surely been misapplied and abused by advocates of the prosperity gospel (see the discussion in chapter 3), Jesus did allude to the possibility of material increase for His disciples as He taught, "There is no one who has left house . . . or lands, for my sake and for the gospel, who will not receive a hundredfold now in this time . . . and in the age to come . . ." (Mark 10:29–30).[27]

It would be difficult to demonstrate that Jesus favored either the possession of wealth or a state of poverty in His practice and teaching, at least not to the exclusion of the opposing condition. In fact, a survey of the Gospels reveals that while economic matters frequently arose in Christ's life and ministry, He gave no systematic, detailed economic plan to His followers. Rather, Jesus' example and teachings on wealth and poverty are wide-ranging and their spiritual impact is what is usually emphasized. The economic citations from Christ's life and ministry are, in fact, often peripheral to the main point of the narratives in which they occur. This fact notwithstanding, though, it is possible to summarize the main emphases of Jesus' economic ethic with two broad observations from His teaching.

First, a major theme in Jesus' life related to wealth and poverty is the duty of believers to care for those who are impoverished. Interestingly, while the creation ideal of laboring is not stressed in the Gospels,[28] the Old Testament emphasis on caring for the poor is readily apparent in the ministry of Christ. Poverty itself is not presented in the Gospels—or anywhere in Scripture, for that matter—as being inherently sinful. During His incarnation, Jesus was relatively poor, at times voluntarily so, yet was without sin (see 2 Cor. 5:21; Heb. 4:15). However, the Bible does recognize the causes and effects of poverty to be oftentimes sinful. Therefore, believers ought to work to alleviate involuntary poverty, for doing so is both Christlike and in accord with the gospel.

Note that Jesus began His ministry by quoting Isaiah 61:1, "The Spirit of the Lord God is upon me, because the Lord has anointed me to bring good news to the poor" (see Luke 4:18), and during His earthly ministry, this was Christ's example. When believers care for the poor, they imitate Jesus and in doing so effectively minister to Him (see Matt. 25:31–46).[29] Such ministry is a fulfillment and depiction of God's plan of redemption, which aims at the restoration of all things (see Acts 3:21; Rom. 8:21), including proper stewardship over material resources. While there will always be involuntary poverty before the return of the Lord (see Mark 14:7),[30] laboring in order to meet the needs of the poor is a duty of members of the body of Christ.

A second recurring theme in the economic teachings of Christ is that wealth can be a spiritual stumbling block. Believers need to be on guard against the temptations of material wealth. This complements the notion of caring for the poor, for if wealth is not idolized, then ministering to the needy becomes a natural application of right stewardship. This theme is evident in one of Jesus' most well-known economic statements—His reflection upon interacting with the rich, young, ruler, "Truly, I say to you, only with difficulty will a rich person enter the kingdom of heaven" (Matt. 19:23). Contextually it seems that this was not intended to be a univocal statement about the necessary evils of material wealth; rather, it is Christ's evaluation of the character of the rich, young ruler—a man whose actions showed that he valued material status above his own spiritual well-being.[31] The theme of wealth as a potential spiritual stumbling block is also demonstrable in that as Jesus traveled about Israel calling His disciples, it was common for them to voluntarily leave their material goods in order to follow Him (see Matt. 19:27; Mark 1:18; 10:28). This appears to be a prerequisite, of sorts, for all of Jesus' followers, for when instructing a great crowd outside of Jerusalem, Christ taught, "Any one of you who does not renounce all that he has cannot be my disciple" (Luke 14:33).

While there are numerous examples of individuals in the Gospels for whom wealth was a spiritual stumbling block—ranging from the Pharisees "who were lovers of money" (Luke 16:14), to the money changers in the temple (see Matt. 21:12–13), to Judas Iscariot (see Matt. 26:14–16; John 12:4–6)—Jesus' warnings about the trappings of wealth ought not to be seen as a complete ban on the accumulation and enjoyment of material goods. As already noted, in His life and ministry Christ Himself benefited from the wealth of others and even instructed His disciples in the use of material goods for their own spiritual pursuits (see Luke 22:35–36).[32] Wealthy individuals—including Zacchaeus and Joseph of Arimathea— followed Jesus, and others—such as the Gerasene demoniac—desired to leave all in order to follow Jesus, but were prohibited from doing so by Christ Himself (see Mark 5:18–19). Jesus' warnings about wealth being a spiritual stumbling block are given as a sobering admonition, but they should not be broadened beyond their intended application. Perhaps a good summary of this economic theme in Jesus' teaching are His words in the Sermon on the Mount, "Do not lay up for yourselves treasures on earth . . . but lay up for yourselves treasures in heaven . . . for where your treasure is, there your heart will be also" (Matt. 6:19–21).

ACTS AND THE EPISTLES

In a similar manner to the Prophets and Writings in the Old Testament, the book of Acts and the Epistles in the New Testament record the moral successes and failures of God's people. Concerning economics, the familiar ideals of laboring and caring for the poor, as well as the warning about wealth being a potential spiritual stumbling block, are all present.

Given the lack of emphasis placed on laboring in the Gospels, it is surprising to note the regularity with which this creation ideal is appealed to in the Epistles. The duty to work is frequently mentioned by Paul, as the apostle understood laboring to meet material needs to be a normal part of the Christian life. Paul writes, "Let the thief no longer steal, but rather let him labor, doing honest work with his own hands" (Eph. 4:28), and "But we urge you, brothers . . . to work with your hands, as we instructed you" (1 Thess. 4:10–11). Paul not only believes honest work to be incumbent upon believers but also that labor is a means of meeting material needs, for "the laborer deserves his wages" (1 Tim. 5:18; see Matt. 10:10; Luke 10:7).

Paul teaches that labor affords workers an opportunity to meet the needs of the poor. Paul exhorts the Ephesians to work, in part, so that they would "have something to share with anyone in need" (Eph. 4:28). The apostle frequently holds himself up as a model in this regard. In the book of Acts, Paul reminds the church at Miletus, "In all things I have shown you that by working hard in this way we must help the weak" (Acts 20:35; see 1 Cor. 4:12; 9:6; 1 Thess. 2:9).[33] Paul's emphasis on labor can be seen in his repeated warnings against idleness, such as, "If anyone is not willing to work, let him not eat" (2 Thess. 3:10).

James exhorts his readers with the teaching, "Religion that is pure and undefiled before God, the Father, is this: to visit orphans and widows in their affliction" (James 1:27). The apostle Paul's example aligns with James's words—he was someone who aided the poor. This is evident in the apostle's day-to-day ministry, as well as in the periodic benevolence offerings that he received and distributed from the churches to whom he ministered (see Rom. 15:25–28; 1 Cor. 16:1–4; 2 Cor. 8–9).

In the New Testament an often appealed to instance of caring for the poor is the early church's example of communal living. Acts 2:44–45 and 4:32–35 report this event:

And all who believed were together and had all things in common. And they were selling their possessions and belongings and distributing the proceeds to all, as any had need. . . . Now the full number of those who believed were of one heart and soul, and no one said that any of the things that belonged to him was his own, but they had everything in common. And with great power the apostles were giving their testimony to the resurrection of the

Lord Jesus, and great grace was upon them all. There was not a needy person among them, for as many as were owners of lands or houses sold them and brought the proceeds of what was sold and laid it at the apostles' feet, and it was distributed to each as any had need.

Given the positive presentation and results of this communal living in the Jerusalem church, it is understandable that some throughout church history have viewed this situation to be normative for the Christian life. Several factors make this conclusion unlikely. First it should be noted that Acts 2:44–45 and 4:32–35 are narrative passages, not prescriptive passages. Viewing the wide-ranging narrative passages of Scripture as normative for the Christian opens up a Pandora's Box of interpretation and risks confusing principle with application. Additionally, there are numerous passages and examples in the Bible that contradict the notion of communal living being a requirement for believers. These passages include Matthew 25:14–30; Acts 5:4; 2 Corinthians 8:1–9:15; and 2 Thessalonians 3:7–10. Rather than viewing Acts 2:44–45 and 4:32–35 as normative for the Christian life, then, it seems better to understand this situation in the life of the early church to be an application of the principle of caring for the poor. In other words, many in the early church were impoverished; therefore, members of the body of Christ simply pooled their resources to meet the needs of their brothers and sisters. It was a contextual application of the gospel, not a timeless moral principle or a prescription for a specific political or economic system.[34]

Finally, the gospel teaching that wealth can be a spiritual stumbling block is also present in the book of Acts and in the Epistles. This theme can be seen in the most well-known, and likely the most misquoted, of Paul's teachings about finances: "For the love of money is a root of all kinds of evils. It is through this craving that some have wandered away from the faith and pierced themselves with many pangs" (1 Tim. 6:10). The apostle continues, "As for the rich in this present age, charge them not to be haughty, nor to set their hopes on the uncertainty of riches, but on God, who richly provides us with everything to enjoy. They are to do good, to be rich in good works, to be generous and ready to share, thus storing up treasure for themselves as a good foundation for the future, so that they may take hold of that which is truly life" (1 Tim. 6:17–19). Clearly, as Jesus does in the Gospels, Paul warns about the spiritual pitfalls that accompany the love of money, not about the evils of money itself.

One other way that the theme of wealth being a potential spiritual stumbling block can be seen in the book of Acts and in the Epistles is in the warnings about coveting and greed. These books contain many explicit warnings about coveting, such as, "Keep your life free from love of money, and be content with what you have" (Heb. 13:5), as well as many examples of those who were guilty of this sin. These include Ananias and his wife (see Acts 5:1–10), Simon Magus (see Acts 8:18–23), the owners of the slave girl from whom Paul exorcized a demon (see Acts 16:19), Demetrius the silversmith (see Acts 19:24–27), Felix (see Acts 24:26), and Demas (see 2 Tim. 4:10). These examples and the contexts in which they occur yield the same conclusion that Paul communicates in Ephesians 5:5, "For you may be sure of this, that everyone . . . who is covetous (that is, an idolater), has no inheritance in the kingdom of Christ and God."[35] The sin of covetousness both disqualifies one from ministry (see 1 Tim. 3:3) and is a mark of end-times apostasy (see 2 Tim. 3:2; 2 Peter 2:1–3).[36]

SYNTHESIS

The preceding biblical survey has revealed three major economic themes in Scripture. First, according to the creation narrative, labor is good. Through laboring, people functionally bear God's image and meet their material needs. Second, the Lord's followers are to minister to the poor. This ideal is seen in the Hebrew law and is a major emphasis in the Gospels. To care for the poor is Christlike and a manifestation of the authenticity of one's relationship with the Lord. Third, wealth can be a spiritual stumbling block. While material goods are not inherently evil, wealth is surely one of the greatest idols that people pursue. Members of the community of faith must watch carefully for this spiritual pitfall.

These three economic themes are integrally related. If one labors and generates wealth, then resources will be available to meet the needs of the poor. If material resources are employed in ministering to those who are impoverished, then wealth will not become a spiritual stumbling block. But if wealth becomes a spiritual stumbling block (even wealth gained by honest labor), then one is unlikely to use material resources—at least not in a proportionately sufficient amount—to meet the needs of the poor.

Neither wealth nor poverty is specifically commended or condemned in Scripture. Practically speaking, while biblical ideals assist one in Christian living, the absence of explicit moral categorization of wealth and poverty invites the question of the proper relationship between material wealth/poverty and spiritual wealth/poverty, especially for followers of Christ. This is an important issue, for a right understanding of the relationship between material wealth/poverty and spiritual wealth/poverty can provide both motivation and a general framework for one's economic ethic. An incorrect understanding of the dynamics of this relationship may lead one to embrace false teaching.

There are four possible ways in which to connect material wealth/poverty and spiritual wealth/poverty. First, material wealth can be connected to spiritual wealth. Second, and conversely, there may be a tie between material poverty and spiritual poverty. Third, material poverty may be connected to spiritual wealth. Fourth, the opposite of this would be to posit a tie between material wealth and spiritual poverty. The historical record has shown that to insist upon a *requisite* connection in any of these relational dynamics leads to a departure from orthodox theology. Insisting on a tie between material wealth and spiritual wealth is to espouse the prosperity gospel; connecting material poverty and spiritual poverty is to be guilty of the error of Job's friends; linking material poverty with spiritual wealth makes one an ascetic; and, finally, connecting material wealth and spiritual poverty is to be guilty of materialism.

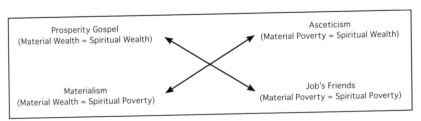

The error of all of these departures from orthodoxy is not that they recognize a connection between material wealth/poverty and spiritual wealth/poverty; rather, it is that they insist upon a *requisite* connection. Given that neither wealth nor poverty is explicitly commended or condemned in Scripture, it is better to conclude that while there can be a tie between material wealth/poverty and spiritual wealth/poverty, any such connection is *nonrequisite*. Rather than claiming—as proponents of the prosperity gospel do—that material wealth is a barometer of spiritual wealth, it is better simply to recognize that on account of the moral traits that accompany spiritual wealth (industry, honesty, diligence, etc.), material wealth often follows. Yet, this is not a quid pro quo transaction. It may be that a spiritually wealthy person is in a low paying job, gets laid off, is cheated, becomes ill, or simply chooses to divest him- or herself of wealth to meet the needs of the poor, as did Christ. The same could be said for any of these four relational dynamics.

CONCLUSION

A study of the biblical teaching on wealth and poverty makes clear that the prosperity gospel is not the biblical gospel. Whereas the biblical gospel encourages people to work in order to meet their needs, the prosperity gospel emphasizes the conjuring of mystical forces of faith in order to meet material needs; whereas the biblical gospel stresses focusing on the material needs of others, especially those who are impoverished, the prosperity gospel focuses on acquiring wealth for oneself; and finally, whereas the biblical gospel warns people about the spiritual pitfalls of accumulated wealth, the prosperity gospel is consumed with the accumulation of wealth. The prosperity gospel is no gospel at all.

SUMMARY POINTS

- One of the best defenses against the teachings of the prosperity gospel is a holistic understanding of scriptural teaching on wealth and poverty.

- God created people with material needs, as well as both the desire and the ability to meet those needs.
- The Old Testament economic laws are built upon the ideals of laboring and resting, as well as preventing God's people from wealth and poverty related sins.
- Jesus gave no systematic, detailed economic plan; rather, in the Gospels, His example and teachings on wealth and poverty are wide-ranging and their spiritual impact is what is usually emphasized.
- There is a nonrequisite connection between material wealth/poverty and spiritual wealth/poverty.

Chapter 6

The Biblical Teaching
on Giving

The prosperity gospel emphasizes the attainment of wealth, health, and general success in life. This emphasis is so great that even the secular media have taken notice. The September 2006 cover of *Time Magazine* asked, "Does God Want You to Be Rich?" More recently *The New York Times* titled its coverage of a gathering of the prosperity gospel faithful at the 2009 Southwest Believers' Convention, "Believers Invest in the Gospel of Getting Rich." A common denominator in these two articles, as well as in other secular treatments of the prosperity gospel, is a questioning of the motive, message, and methodology of the prosperity gospel. In other words, even the secular media sense that something is askew with the idea of giving to God solely for the purpose of getting material blessings from Him. Such a message goes against the grain of historic Christianity.

The problems with the prosperity gospel invite several questions regarding the biblical teaching on giving. We will examine three: Why should Christians give? How much should Christians give? and To whom should Christians give?

WHY SHOULD CHRISTIANS GIVE?

Being a faithful steward is a formidable challenge for every Christian living in a materialistic, consumption-driven society. Many believers are not even familiar with the concept of stewardship. In the New Testament, the term "stewardship" (*oikonomia*) combines the Greek words for "house" (*oikos*) and "command" (*nomos*). The term *oikonomia* primarily denotes a manager who was employed by an owner and commanded to govern the affairs of his household (Luke 16:1–8; 12:42; Gal. 4:2). Speaking more broadly, Christians have been charged by God to steward the material world that He has made (see Gen. 1:28–30). As managers of the created order, Christians are to faithfully steward that which has been entrusted to them by the Lord. One aspect of managing God's resources is giving, and the Bible provides several motivations for His people to give.

Giving Is an Act of Obedience

First, giving is an act of obedience to God. Christians are obligated to give from that with which they have been entrusted. In the Old Testament, God established a particular system of giving under the Mosaic Law called tithing. This system consisted of several different tithes that entailed giving a tenth of one's material increase, including agricultural products, livestock, grain, wine, oil, and other material goods.

The first tithe was for the Levites—the priests—of Israel (see Lev. 27:30–34; Num. 18:21–32; Neh. 10:37–38). These men offered the daily sacrifices to God for the sins of the people. In return for the priests' service, God commanded the Israelites to tithe to provide for the Levites' material needs. The second tithe was called the festival tithe (see Deut. 12:11–12; 14:22–27). In Deuteronomy 14:22–27 God instructed Israel to tithe from the yield of their fields at the central sanctuary so they could worship in the presence of the Lord there. If the distance to the tabernacle/temple was too far, the people could exchange their tithe for money and purchase material goods at the place of the festival (see Deut. 14:25–26). The third tithe was the poor tithe, the welfare tithe (see Deut. 14:28–29; 26:12). This tithe was collected every three years and was distributed to the Levites, foreigners, orphans, and widows. In the Old Testament, God commanded the Israelites to give to support the Levites, to facilitate worship before the Lord, and to support the needy in society.

In the New Testament, God commanded Christians to give in order to assist believers, strangers, and the poor. The apostle Paul reminds Timothy to instruct the rich "to do good, to be rich in good works, to be generous and ready to share" (1 Tim. 6:18). Though the apostle John does not explicitly command the readers of his epistles to give, he could not imagine a Christian not giving to a brother in need, because to do so indicated a lack of love for God (see 1 John 3:17–18). Christians are to demonstrate their faith and love for others through their deeds, including financial benevolence. As James writes, "Religion that is pure and undefiled before God, the Father, is this: to visit orphans and widows in their affliction, . . . So also faith by itself, if it does not have works, is dead" (James 1:27; 2:17). Giving is an act of obedience.

> **Christians are to demonstrate their faith and love for others through their deeds, including financial benevolence.**

Giving Demonstrates Love

A second motivation for giving is love for God and love for others. In the words of Christ, the first and greatest commandment is, "You shall love the Lord your God with all your heart and with all your soul and with all your mind. . . . And a second is like it: You shall love your neighbor as yourself" (Matt. 22:37, 39). The apostle John writes that Christians are to love God and others because He loved us first, noting that it is impossible to love God and not love one's brother (see 1 John 4:19–21). One way that believers can manifest such love is to give of their possessions for God's work, thereby meeting the material needs of others.

A common practical example in the Bible of loving others is the act of providing aid to fellow disciples and showing hospitality. In his letter to the church in Rome, the apostle Paul encourages believers to "contribute to the needs of the saints and seek to show hospitality" (Rom. 12:13). When he was sent to minister among the Gentiles, Paul himself declares that he was eager to assist the poor (see Gal. 2:10). In a similar manner the author of the book of Hebrews writes, "Do not neglect to do good and to share what you have, for such sacrifices are pleasing to God" (Heb. 13:16).

John also echoes the theme of helping others in need as he encourages Christians to demonstrate both their love and their faith. John rhetorically asks, "But if anyone has the world's goods and sees his brother in need, yet closes his heart against him, how does God's love abide in him?" (1 John 3:17). Clearly believers are to be motivated by love—not, as the prosperity gospel teaches, a desire for personal flourishing—and should realize that when they help those in need they are, in effect, ministering to the Lord (see Prov. 19:17; Matt. 25:34–36). Just as Jesus gave His life out of love to help those in need, so Christians are to do likewise.

Giving Brings Glory to God

A third motivation for giving is to bring glory to God. Christians ought to use their possessions to show the world that God and His kingdom are more important than the things of this world. When believers give generously to help others, people will glorify God in response. Jesus teaches His listeners to obey so that the watching world will "see your good works and give glory to your Father who is in heaven" (Matt. 5:16). John reiterates this truth when he writes, "By this my Father is glorified, that you bear much fruit and so prove to be my disciples" (John 15:8). Likewise, Peter encourages his readers, "Keep your conduct among the Gentiles honorable, so that when they speak against you as evildoers, they may see your good deeds and glorify God on the day of visitation" (1 Peter 2:12). In Paul's second letter to the Corinthian church, he anticipates that the believers in Jerusalem will glorify God because of the Corinthian church's obedience in taking a benevolence offering. Paul writes, "By their approval of this service, they will glorify God because of your submission flowing from your confession of the gospel of Christ, and the generosity of your contribution for them and for all others" (2 Cor. 9:13; see 1 Cor. 10:31). From these verses, it is clear that one goal of giving is to bring glory to God.

Giving Is a Result of the Gospel

A fourth motivation for giving is the gospel itself. A proper under-standing of the gospel will motivate Christians to give. When the gos-pel takes root in people's lives, their view of ownership changes. Often Christians live with the illusion that what they possess actually belongs to them. The truth, however, is that God is the sole owner of all things. In the book of Psalms, God says, "The world and everything in it is Mine" (Ps. 50:12 HCSB), and the prophet Haggai records the Lord's declaration, "The silver and gold belong to Me" (Hag. 2:8 HCSB). David explained that God, the creator of the universe, is the ultimate source of riches, honor, and power (see 1 Chron. 29:11–12). Therefore, the role of the Christian is to acknowledge God's ownership of all things and to be a faithful stew-ard of the Lord's resources.

> **Christians ought to use their possessions
> to show the world that God and His kingdom are more
> important than the things of this world.**

The gospel changes people, and generosity is one of the best indica-tors of the condition of the heart. Jesus understood this principle well. On His way through Jericho, Jesus called out to a wealthy tax collec-tor named Zacchaeus (see Luke 19:1–10). Before Zacchaeus had time to ponder how the Lord knew his name, Jesus announced His intent to dine with him. Later, in the presence of Jesus, Zacchaeus promised to give away half of his possessions and repay anyone he had cheated. After this announcement, Jesus said, "Today salvation has come to this house, since he also is a son of Abraham. For the Son of Man came to seek and to save the lost" (Luke 19:9–10). Notice that the external proof of Zac-chaeus's salvation was his generosity. For Zacchaeus, giving reflected the reality of a new heart that loved Jesus more than wealth.

The Bible speaks often about possessions because God knows that His children can become enamored with the things of this world. A person's finances, abilities, and time all compete with God for worship. People cannot love both God and money because God cannot share His glory. Jesus makes this clear, teaching, "No household slave can be the slave of two masters, since either he will hate one and love the other, or he will be devoted to one and despise the other. You can't be slaves to both God and money" (Luke 16:13 HCSB). Reflecting on this passage in his book *The Cost of Discipleship*, Dietrich Bonhoeffer writes, "If our hearts are entirely given to God, it is clear that we cannot serve two masters; it is simply impossible—at any rate all the time we are following Christ. . . . Our hearts have room for only one all-embracing devotion, and we can only cleave to one Lord."[1]

Jesus not only talks about money competing with God for our attention, but He also makes an explicit connection between our love for God, our heart, and our possessions. He says, "For where your treasure is, there your heart will be also" (Matt. 6:21). His point is that what you value most shows what or whom you love most. Where you spend your time, abilities, and money reflects what you think is most important in life. Your checkbooks, calendars, and activities are theological statements about what you treasure most. We show by the use of our resources that God and the gospel are far more important than wealth. Giving is an external reflection of the internal condition of one's heart.

When the gospel of grace takes root, one's view of eternity changes. Christians' true citizenship and destiny is in the new heavens and new earth (see Phil. 3:20). This does not mean that believers ought to neglect their responsibilities in the here-and-now. The church has been charged with bringing the gospel to this world. In other words, Christians should not be like the successful man in Jesus' parable who built bigger barns in order to make his life more secure (see Luke 12:13–21). Christ called this man a fool for such presumptuous thinking, for the man was going to die that night. The meaning of Jesus' parable is this: those who store up earthly treasure for themselves and place their confidence in such, rather than in God, are fools. Certainly, hoarding money is not an option for the Christian.

John Calvin observed, "[W]here riches hold the dominion of the heart, God has lost all authority. True, it is not impossible that those who are rich shall serve God; but whoever gives himself up as a slave to riches must abandon the service of God: for covetousness makes us the slaves of the devil."[2] When we pursue the things of this world, they distract us from our pursuit of God. Randy Alcorn, in his book *Money, Possessions, and Eternity*, correctly points out that materialism consists of the two things God hates most: idolatry and adultery.[3] We replace God with the things of His creation, and we flirt with the things of this world to gain satisfaction. Instead of finding acceptance in the gospel, we build up our earthly possessions to gain the acceptance of people. The gospel, however, frees us from finding security and safety in things of this world.

Giving Results in Reward

A fifth motivation for giving is reward. At face value, rewards as motivation may appear selfish, but Scripture itself provides this motivation. Jesus Christ will judge every believer for faithful stewardship at the judgment seat (see 1 Cor. 3:12–15; 2 Cor. 5:10). Rewards will be distributed to those who faithfully managed what God gave them, including their gifts, time, and possessions. While exact details are sparse in Scripture, heavenly rewards will apparently consist of crowns and differing levels of responsibilities in heaven (see Luke 19:16–19; 2 Tim. 4:8). This concept of giving on account of heavenly rewards must be distinguished from the prosperity gospel. Erwin Lutzer, pastor of Moody Church in Chicago, explains, "Of course, the works we do after our conversion do not have merit in and of themselves; they have merit because we are joined to Christ. He takes our imperfect works and makes them acceptable to the Father. Also, we should not think that God must pay us like an employer who has a legal obligation to pay his employee. . . . Our good deeds are done only because God gives us the desire and ability to do them. They are a gift of his grace to us."[4]

Certainly the concept of rewards is biblical, but the question remains as to whether or not these rewards are spiritual or material in nature. The prosperity gospel argues that rewards are primarily material and received on earth, but the Bible stresses the spiritual nature of rewards. The Scriptures teach that we can be rewarded for being persecuted on behalf of

Christ (see Luke 6:23), for working diligently for our employer (see Col. 3:23–24), for loving our enemies (see Luke 6:35), for helping the poor (see Luke 14:12–14), for general good works (see Matt. 6:1), and for faith in God (Heb. 11:6). In each of these examples, the nature of the reward is spiritual and awaits the believer in the new heavens and new earth.

Christians can also be rewarded for generous giving. In writing about a future benevolence offering, Paul reminds the Corinthians, "Whoever sows sparingly will also reap sparingly, and whoever sows bountifully will also reap bountifully" (2 Cor. 9:6). Likewise, Paul instructs Timothy to remind the wealthy to set their hopes on God, rather than on their earthly wealth. Timothy was to encourage the wealthy to "do good, to be rich in good works, to be generous and ready to share, thus storing up treasure for themselves as a good foundation for the future, so that they may take hold of that which is truly life" (1 Tim. 6:18–19). In a similar manner, Jesus exhorts His followers to focus on storing up treasures in heaven rather than on the earth (see Matt. 6:19–20). Earthly treasures are temporary and empty, while heavenly treasures are eternal and fulfilling.

There are major differences between the biblical promises of rewards for giving and the prosperity gospel. The prosperity gospel emphasizes rewards as if they were the only motivation for giving, and it views rewards primarily as present and material in nature, as opposed to future and spiritual. This false gospel turns God's grace into a law that He must obey. While God does sometimes reward believers with financial blessings, He is not obligated to do so. Christians ought to give to God out of a loving heart knowing that He will reward as He sees fit. Contrary to the message of prosperity theology, the concept of rewards in Scripture primarily focuses on spiritual blessings in the new heavens and new earth, not on personal flourishing in the here-and-now.

HOW MUCH SHOULD CHRISTIANS GIVE?

On November 23, 2007, *The Wall Street Journal* published an article titled "The Backlash Against Tithing." The article publicized the growing debate among evangelicals about the legitimacy of tithing for today's Christian. On March 2, 2008, CBS News *Sunday Morning* aired a segment that they labeled "To Tithe or Not to Tithe?" It examined whether giving 10 percent of one's income to the church is applicable to today's Christian. Without a doubt, the discussion and debate about tithing among evangelicals is becoming more prominent.[5] While evangelicals may disagree about whether the tithe is binding for Christians today, all agree that generous giving is a biblical mandate.

Generous giving is a biblical mandate.

Giving Before the Mosaic Law

In the Old Testament, the discussion of giving centers on the concept of tithing, which was the most often used formal methodology of giving within the Hebrew theocracy. However, two passages mention the tithe prior to the giving of the Mosaic Law—Genesis 14:17–20 and Genesis 28:20–22. In the first passage, after victory in battle, Abraham (Abram) voluntarily gave a tithe of the spoils of war to the priest Melchizedek, perhaps as an expression of gratitude. An argument can be made that since Abraham gave a tenth before the Law, tithing should be considered normative apart from the Mosaic Law. A problem with this argument, however, is that Abraham gave a tenth of the property that he had recovered from the war (see Heb. 7:4). Abraham tithed off other people's goods, not his own income. This act of giving appears to be a single occurrence. No evidence in the biblical narrative suggests that God commanded this tithe or that Abraham regularly tithed of his own income.

In the second passage, Genesis 28:20–22, Jacob, fleeing from his brother Esau, made a vow to tithe to God in response to a dream. In the dream, God promised Jacob land, offspring, safety, and that He would be with Jacob (see Gen. 28:13–15). Jacob apparently doubted God's promises and told God that if He would grant him safety, provide food and clothing, and bring him back to his father's house in peace, then the Lord would be his God. Jacob also promised God a tenth of his increase. While God fulfilled His promises, when Jacob returned to Bethel two decades later, there is no mention of him tithing (see Gen. 35:1–15). As with the account of Abraham and Melchizedek, it is difficult to develop a clear ethic of tithing from the narrative of Jacob's flight from and return to Canaan.

Giving Under the Mosaic Law

Within the Mosaic Law, numerous passages address and prescribe formal giving for God's people. Most of these involve tithing. The Mosaic Law specified three different types of tithes that were to be practiced by the Israelites. The first was for the support of the Levites of Israel. This tithe enabled the Levites to minister at the tabernacle/temple in a full-time capacity. The second tithe was the festival tithe. This tithe prompted the people to travel to Jerusalem in order to worship God. The third tithe was known as the poor or welfare tithe. This third tithe was collected every three years and was to be distributed to the needy Levites, foreigners, orphans, and widows.

Based on these three different tithes, each family annually gave at least 20 percent of their goods to the Lord, with an extra 10 percent every third year. This does not include other giving specified in the Mosaic Law, such as the tabernacle/temple tax, gleaning rights, sacrificial offerings, and other forms of benevolence (see Exod. 30:11–16; Lev. 19:9–10; 2 Chron. 24:6–10; Neh. 10:32–33; Matt. 17:24–27). John MacArthur observed, "So the Jews were required to provide a Levites' tithe, a festivals tithe, a poor (welfare) tithe, a profit-sharing tax, the every-seventh-year land Sabbath, and the temple tax. All of that calculates out to more than 25 percent in annual income tax to the theocratic government of Israel."[6]

Giving After the Mosaic Law

Many Old Testament passages after the Mosaic Law mention giving, yet most focus upon calling God's people back to the standards of giving (i.e., tithing) prescribed in the Law. Likely the most often cited of these passages is Malachi 3:8–10. This passage reads, "Will man rob God? Yet you say, 'How have we robbed you?' In your tithes and contributions. You are cursed with a curse, for you are robbing me, the whole nation of you. Bring the full tithes into the storehouse, that there may be food in my house. And thereby put me to the test, says the LORD of hosts, if I will not open the windows of heaven for you and pour down for you a blessing until there is no more need."

While it may be tempting to use this passage to insist that contemporary believers give 10 percent, one must keep in mind the context of Malachi 3:8–10. Malachi is an Old Testament prophet confronting the nation of Israel for their violation of the Mosaic Law. Malachi 3:8–10 is a call to repentance from the sin of wandering from God. As Andrew Hill notes, "By calling for the full tithe the prophet invites genuine repentance, a return to God with the whole heart."[7] In other words, the failure to give was an external symbol of Israel's internal spiritual bankruptcy.[8] A valid principle from this text is that one's giving can be used to measure one's love and devotion to God. If a person is generous in giving toward God's work, it reflects positively on that person's spiritual maturity. If one neglects giving, it demonstrates a lack of love or worship toward God. This application reflects God's desire for worship and is a timeless principle that is repeated in the New Testament.

Giving in the New Testament

Somewhat surprisingly, the New Testament does not appear to prescribe a formal method or amount of giving for Christians. While some have argued that tithing ought to be considered normative for contemporary believers, only three passages in the New Testament mention the tithe: Matthew 23:23, Luke 18:12, and Hebrews 7:1–10.[9] In Matthew 23:23, Jesus rebuked the Pharisees for tithing of their spices but ignoring more important matters such as justice, mercy, and faithfulness. This verse, however, provides little help for a discussion of tithing, because the Pharisees were not Christians but Jews under the Mosaic Law.

In Luke 18:9–14 Jesus tells a parable about a self-righteous Pharisee and a humble tax collector who were offering prayers in the temple. In his prayer the Pharisee boasted of his good works, his tithing, and his fasting, while the tax collector beat his chest and asked God for mercy. Given that Christ's purpose in this parable was to teach what true humility before God entails, this passage yields little information about giving. The reference to tithing in this passage is largely incidental and is also applied to a Jewish Pharisee living under the Mosaic Law.

A final mention of tithing is in Hebrews 7:1–10. In this passage, the author of Hebrews makes the case that Jesus is a priest after the order of Melchizedek. The author argues that Melchizedek's priesthood was superior to the Levitical priesthood and, therefore, Jesus' priesthood is superior to that of Levi. The main point of this passage is not to teach about tithing. New Testament scholars Köstenberger and Croteau write, "If anyone were to prove the continuation of tithing based upon the New Testament, he must produce a passage that has as its primary purpose that goal in mind. If such a passage is produced, then Heb. 7 could possibly be utilized as a secondary, supporting statement. The important point to remember is this: the author of Hebrews was arguing for Melchizedek's superiority over the Levitical priesthood."[10]

The New Testament, then, is fairly silent in regard to tithing. In their various writings, Paul, Peter, John, and Jude do not mention the tithe. Some may argue that since the tithe is never revoked in the New Testament, it still applies. This conclusion rests upon answers to questions about the application of the Old Testament law in the New Testament—questions that fall beyond the scope of this book.

Generous giving is a tangible expression of our love for God.

Regardless of one's view of tithing, evangelicals generally agree that for most believers, giving generously to one's local church is a good place to start. While the New Testament does not appear to prescribe a formal, legalistic method or amount of giving for believers, it does provide several principles of giving that most evangelicals embrace despite different views of tithing—principles that ought to encourage many to give more than 10 percent.

Principles for Giving

Two of the most pointed passages in the New Testament that address giving occur in Paul's letters to the Corinthian church. The first is in 1 Corinthians 16:1–2, where the apostle writes, "Now concerning the collection for the saints: as I directed the churches of Galatia, so you also are to do. On the first day of every week, each of you is to put something aside and store it up, as he may prosper, so that there will be no collecting when I come." The second passage, which is too lengthy to quote here in its entirety, covers all of 2 Corinthians 8–9. Using 1 Corinthians 16:2 as a rubric, five principles of giving can be distilled from these two passages.

First, giving is to be *periodic*. Paul writes to the Corinthians, "On the first day of every week . . ." (1 Cor. 16:2). There is ample biblical evidence that the early church met weekly, on Sunday (see John 20:26; Acts 20:7; Heb. 4:9–10; Rev. 1:10). Paul begins his instructions about giving by noting that the Corinthian Christians should give when they were gathered together each week. Such giving would prevent a lack when funds were needed (see 2 Cor. 8:10–14; 9:3–5). In modern times some believers are not compensated weekly, but even if one were paid on a monthly basis, giving could still be periodic.

Second, giving is to be *personal*. Paul continues his instructions to the Corinthians by directing, "[let] each of you . . ." (1 Cor. 16:2). Every Christian ought to give, for generous giving is a personal response to receiving God's indescribable gift, Jesus Christ (see 2 Cor. 8:1–2, 9; 9:15). God gave His only Son to atone for sin, to reconcile man to God, and to grant eternal life to those who repent and believe. Jesus came to earth so that we might become eternally rich through faith in Him (see 2 Cor. 8:9). God's grace toward us becomes a motivation for giving, and generous giving is a tangible expression of our love for God.

Third, giving is to be *planned*. Paul directs the Corinthians, "Put something aside and store it up" (1 Cor. 16:2). The apostle is calling for thought and intention in regard to giving. Paul does not make an emotional plea by giving heart-wrenching stories, he does not appeal to guilt, nor does he endorse sporadic, impulse-type giving. In the epistle of 2 Corinthians, the apostle holds up planned, intentional giving as he refers to giving with "a willing mind" (2 Cor. 8:12 NKJV) and references the gift that the Corinthians had previously promised (see 2 Cor. 9:5).

Fourth, giving is to be *proportionate*. Paul notes that each believer was to give "as he may prosper" (1 Cor. 16:2). Later, in 2 Corinthians 8:3, the apostle encourages the church to give "according to their means." In other words, each person was to give according to what he or she possessed. People with greater wealth could give more than those with less wealth. Paul teaches that readiness and willingness to give are important, writing, "For if the readiness is there, it is acceptable according to what a person has, not according to what he does not have" (2 Cor. 8:12). Giving is predicated upon a right attitude. Paul does not want believers to give out of a sense of obligation but proportionately, willingly, and cheerfully (see 2 Cor. 9:7). Note that giving in such a manner is only possible when one understands the gospel and loves God more than earthly possessions.

Fifth, giving is to be *plentiful*. Paul concludes his instruction, ". . . so that there will be no collecting when I come" (1 Cor. 16:2). Generous giving is a sign of spiritual maturity and sincere love. Paul challenges the church to demonstrate the sincerity of their love for their fellow brothers by giving in such a manner so as to meet their needs. In 2 Corinthians 8:7–8 the apostle encourages the church to abound in the grace of giving, just as they abound in faith, speech, and knowledge. Genuine love for God and growth in the Christian life result in a giving heart. A heart dedicated to Christ cannot help but be generous toward God and His people, often leading one to give more than 10 percent.

TO WHOM SHOULD CHRISTIANS GIVE?

In the United States, numerous worthy organizations ask Christians for donations—churches, television ministries, missionary organizations, local charities, local civic groups, educational institutions, and many others. How does one sort through the possibilities and give responsibly in a biblical manner? Surprisingly, Scripture does not specifically direct believers where they ought to give. It does, however, provide wisdom that can guide Christians in their giving. The New Testament reveals three categories for giving.

The first and arguably most important place to give is to the local church. Paul teaches that the elder is worthy of his wages (see Gal. 6:6; 1 Tim. 5:17–18). An elder or pastor can reasonably expect support from the church that he serves. An elder does not have to draw support, however, as he may minister in a bivocational manner and receive little or no support from the church; the apostle Paul chose to engage in the vocation of tent-making rather than draw support from all of the churches to which he ministered (see Acts 18:1–3; 20:33–35; 1 Cor. 9:6, 12, 15; Phil. 4:14–16).

While there is a biblical reason for supporting the church, there are also practical reasons. Most churches require funds to pay for utilities, maintenance, equipment, materials, and the like. More importantly, the local church is the place that ministers to the body of Christ, to the community, and to the world by supporting missionaries, local Christian charities, and those in need in the congregation. By giving to your local church, you also provide funds for local evangelistic outreaches and other ministries that serve the community. In the end, you know that your money is going to support a doctrinally sound church that uses the money wisely. Without question, your local church ought to be your first priority in giving.

Second, you can give to other Christian organizations. This would include mission organizations, parachurch groups, and individuals who are involved in these ministries (see 3 John 5–8). Hopefully, your local church and denomination are connected to some of these ministries, but obviously the local church cannot do everything. Therefore, on your own you may desire to support a community pregnancy support center, a ministry for orphans, or a friend who will be serving overseas. A word of caution, however, is that giving to other Christian organizations ought not to usurp the place of the church. Too often, other organizations and ministries compete for our giving, and if we are not careful, our church is neglected. Unfortunately, this happens all too often with television-based prosperity gospel ministries. People give more to a televangelist whom they watch once a week than they do to their local church. Such a paradigm for giving is not wise.

Third, it is important to give to those who are in need. This includes both believers and unbelievers who have genuine material needs. The Bible is clear that the community of faith is to assist the poor. We are to be wise but open to using what God has given us to meet the needs of those in our church and community (see Gal. 6:10; 2 Thess. 3:6–10; Heb. 10:32–34; 13:1–3; James 2:15–16; 1 John 3:17).

Regardless of how much is given, it is important to give to ministries that exalt Christ and that exhibit transparency in their financial dealings. In the United States, most reputable Christian organizations belong to the Evangelical Council for Financial Accountability (ECFA). While certainly not foolproof, this organization provides accreditation to Christian nonprofit organizations that demonstrate compliance with standard accounting practices. The Web site of the ECFA provides financial information for more than fourteen hundred organizations. To belong to the ECFA, an organization must fully disclose its general financial statements to the public. This requirement ensures transparency and encourages financial integrity. In addition, ECFA members must subscribe to a doctrinal statement that covers the historical, biblical teachings of the Protestant faith.

Another organization that provides financial information for donors is Wall Watchers. One of their programs, Ministry Watch, helps donors identify Christian faith-based charities that demonstrate openness and transparency in their financial matters. Like the ECFA, this organization considers both doctrine and financial dealings in their analysis of various ministries. As a part of their work, Ministry Watch compiles a list of exemplary organizations, as well as a "Donor Alert" list of organizations that do not meet their criteria of financial transparency. Numerous prosperity gospel ministries appeared on the Donor Alert list.[11]

Obviously, a Christian organization that refuses to disclose its financial statements and fails to follow normal accounting practices gives a clear warning sign. While lack of disclosure does not necessarily indicate wrongdoing, donors can never be sure of how the organization spends their money. As Christians, we have a responsibility to God to be good stewards in all areas of finance, including our giving to honest, doctrinally sound ministries. There is no justification for giving to ministries that are promoting heretical doctrine.

CONCLUSION

Prosperity teachers tend to focus their message on the immediate, material rewards for giving. In so doing they promote an unbiblical motive for giving. Rather than focusing on the gospel as the foundation for giving, advocates of the prosperity gospel ask the faithful to give to their ministry in order to receive material blessings. In contrast, when the gospel of Christ is rightly proclaimed, it serves as a catalyst for generous giving that honors God and will result in future spiritual blessings. Though the amount given is not unimportant, a more significant aspect of the act of Christian giving is the attitude of the heart. Indeed, as Paul instructed the Corinthian church, "God loves a cheerful giver" (2 Cor. 9:7). When we give joyfully to the church and to Christian ministries that are faithful to the Word of God, we show our love for God in a tangible way.

SUMMARY POINTS

- Reasons for Christians' giving include obedience, to demonstrate love, to bring glory to God, because it is a result of the gospel, and because it results in reward.
- Contrary to the prosperity gospel, the biblical emphasis is not on present physical rewards for giving but on future spiritual rewards.
- Evangelicals disagree about the concept of tithing, but all agree that generous giving is a biblical mandate.
- Christians ought to faithfully give to the local church, other Christian organizations, and directly to those who are in need.
- Christian nonprofit organizations such as the Evangelical Council for Financial Accountability and Wall Watchers serve as resources to get information about reputable Christian charities and organizations.

Conclusion

This book has sought to demonstrate that the prosperity gospel is a false gospel. It is not the biblical gospel but a modern repackaging of ancient heresies. Yet, the slick presentation and polished message of many of the prosperity preachers, and the Christian veneer that the prosperity gospel is often given, have led many contemporary believers to buy into this false gospel. In fact, the prosperity gospel may be subtly influencing your church, your Christian friends, or even yourself. Since prosperity gospel teachings are pervasive in the church, how do you tell whether you or your loved ones have unwittingly succumbed to false teaching?

THE PROSPERITY GOSPEL: SELF-DIAGNOSIS

Good questions can help us discern what we believe. We would like to suggest and explore five questions that address some of the foundational ideas upon which the prosperity gospel rests. It is our hope that through these queries readers will be able to better discern their own openness to prosperity gospel ideas, as well as to correct previous influence of the prosperity gospel in their lives.

First, *Why does God exist and what does He control in the world?* The Bible teaches that God is eternal and is worthy of glory (see Isa. 43:7; 1 Cor. 10:31). Furthermore, God exercises complete control over the world that He created (see Gen. 1:1; Isa. 48:11). This means that we exist in order to serve and to worship God. The Lord is sovereign and does whatever He pleases to accomplish His purposes (see Isa. 46:8–11). God directs our steps and works all things for good (see Prov. 16:9; Rom. 8:28–30). When you start thinking that God exists in order to serve you and grant your desires, you usurp His place. When you start thinking that you control your own future, then you demote God. Such ideas are at the heart of the prosperity gospel. Within prosperity theology, people are the focal point rather than God.

Second, *What is the purpose of suffering and how do I react when I suffer?* This question is closely related to the first. Does your opinion of God change when a tragedy occurs? The Bible depicts God as sovereign and all-knowing. Conversely, many prosperity gospel teachers teach that God is dependent on people in order to act. When you suffer, do you blame God? When suffering comes, do you think that since you have worked hard to obey God, you do not deserve it? This is precisely the kind of thinking toward which the prosperity gospel is oriented. According to the prosperity gospel, you are in control of your own destiny; thus suffering is an indication of your failure to utilize divinely designed means of blessing. In contrast, the Bible teaches that suffering is an instrument to make you more like Christ and that God is working all things in your life for His purposes (see Rom. 5:1–5; 8:16–18).

Third, ask yourself, *What do I deserve in life?* According to the prosperity gospel, you are entitled to a good life that is marked by good health, beneficial relationships, an abundance of resources, and overall success. But is this actually true? The Bible teaches that if we have food and clothing, we should be content (see 1 Tim. 6:8)—anything beyond this is pure grace. In fact, since all people are sinners, eternal condemnation would be a just reward. Yet, because of God's love and mercy, He sent His Son, Jesus, to die on the cross in the place of humanity, thereby making possible the salvation of all who believe (see Rom. 3:23; 5:8; 10:13). We have been given eternal life and everything else we have in this life by God's grace alone (see 1 Chron. 29:10–13).

Fourth, *Why did God save me?* Did God save you because He needs you on His team? Did God save you so that you could be famous and wealthy? Did God save you so that you can fulfill all of your dreams? No. God saved you on account of His great love for you. God saved you so that you might glorify Him forever and so that He might display His grace for all of eternity (see Isa. 43:25; Eph. 2:4–10). We were rescued to glorify God and to do good works. We did not deserve or earn salvation and this fact alone ought to humble us and cause us to express our gratitude toward God. A major problem with prosperity gospel teaching is that people are encouraged to think too highly of themselves (see Rom. 12:3).

A final diagnostic question is, *Why do I give to God?* What is your motivation to give to the church, to Christian charities, and to those in need? Do you give out of a cheerful heart, or do you expect God to pay you back for your generosity? Do you give to please God, who has given you everything, or do you give in order to see if God will come through for you? Do you give out of guilt and obligation, or do you give out of love? If you give to God in order to get something from Him, then you have adopted a framework similar to that of the prosperity gospel. Such a rationale for giving sets one up for failure and short-circuits the true motivation for giving—grace.

Any of these questions answered incorrectly may betray the influence of the prosperity gospel, or it may be a sign that you are at least open to accepting prosperity theology. Given the prosperity gospel's self-centered message, we should not be surprised to find that such teaching is popular, both inside and outside the walls of the church. If you find yourself buying into the prosperity gospel, or at least being open to its ideals, we encourage you to evaluate the prosperity gospel in the light of Scripture.

THE PROSPERITY GOSPEL: MINISTERING TO OTHERS

While you may reject the prosperity gospel wholeheartedly, you probably know someone who embraces the prosperity gospel and supports these types of ministries. What can you do? By way of lovingly ministering to those who support the prosperity gospel, we suggest the following simple steps.

- First, pray that God will open your friend's eyes to the truth about God. Pray that he or she will be drawn to the Bible to seek answers and not become wrapped up in self-exalting false teaching. Pray

that he or she will be open to talking about the prosperity gospel
with you and with others. Speak the truth in love.

- Second, clearly and purposefully teach your friend the biblical
  gospel. We are not suggesting that all (or any) prosperity gospel
  supporters are not saved; rather, by teaching the biblical gospel,
  you will be able to highlight the differences between the prosperity
  gospel and the gospel of Christ. Show your friend from Scripture
  what God promises to believers. The Lord never promises a successful life by the world's definition but rather eternal life in a new
  heaven and new earth.

- Third, ask questions of your friend aimed at producing dialogue
  about the prosperity gospel. Questions that you might consider
  include, What attracts you to the prosperity gospel? If you lost
  all your money, or health, or friendships, would Jesus be enough?
  How does this particular preacher help you? How would you
  define success? Do you have any doubts about the prosperity gospel? Don't be afraid to answer difficult questions your friend may
  ask with an "I don't know; I'll need to research it and get back to
  you." Use this book as a resource.

- Fourth, use Scripture to guide your conversation. All teaching
  must be judged by the Word of God and not by feelings. Just
  because a preacher promises better days ahead if you have faith,
  does not mean that it is true. Ask your friend to consider the life
  of Christ, Job, and other biblical examples of believers who did
  not experience material prosperity in this life (see Heb. 11:35–39).
  Show your friend some of the erroneous statements that his or her
  favorite preacher has made. Ask your friend to defend his or her
  favorite prosperity belief with Scripture.

- Fifth, give your friend information about the ministries to which
  they send money or follow closely. You can check Wall Watchers at
  www.ministrywatch.com or the Evangelical Council for Financial
  Accountability at www.ecfa.org to get some more information. We
  have also included a list of books that delve deeper into the prosperity gospel in the back of this volume (see "For Further Study").

Throughout this process, God can use your prayers, the gospel, your questions, and His Word to draw your friend to Himself.

Trust that God will use your conversations to help your friend see the truth. With His help you can provide biblical answers.

THE PROSPERITY GOSPEL: OBJECTIONS AND REPLIES

When discussing the prosperity gospel, or perhaps after reading this book, someone may ask, *How can the prosperity gospel be false if so many people follow it?* The objection here is that since tens of thousands of people attend churches that promote the prosperity gospel, the message cannot possibly be wrong. At the heart of this argument is the idea that if enough people believe something to be true, then it must be true.

In response, it can be pointed out that truth cannot be determined by how many people support a particular doctrine or message. Truth must be determined by Scripture. Just because someone believes something to be true does not make it true. For example, just because many sixteenth-century Europeans believed that the earth was the center of the universe did not make it so. Both history and other religions demonstrate that millions of people can be deceived and follow a lie.

Another objection that may arise during discussions about the prosperity gospel is, *But most prosperity gospel teachers seem sincere, and it seems that they genuinely want to help people.* Without a doubt many prosperity teachers seem to want to help people lead better lives. Yet, their message achieves just the opposite, for they do not proclaim the Christ of the Bible. Prosperity teachers may be sincere, yet they can be sincerely wrong. It is possible to be passionate about an issue or problem, but to offer the wrong solution. Sincerity and passion cannot be the standard for evaluating the truth.

Another objection might be, *Everyone does not agree on everything in the Bible. Prosperity theology deserves a place in the church.* As far as the claim that Christians do not agree on everything in the Bible, this is a true statement, but it misses the point. As we have documented in chapters 2 and 3, prosperity gospel teachers promote false teaching about fundamental beliefs such as who God is, the sinfulness and abilities of people, and the way of salvation. These are not insignificant issues. In fact these are core beliefs that either lead to God and to salvation, or away from God and to condemnation. The prosperity gospel is not a harmless movement that is slightly off; rather it is a dangerous movement that has eternal consequences.

Someone may show you a verse in Scripture and claim, *This verse supports the prosperity gospel.* While we have provided refutations of a number of verses in this book (see the Scripture index), prosperity teachers use a wide variety of verses to support their teachings. What can you do? We suggest the following: Carefully look at the verse and examine the context of the passage in which it occurs. Be sure to read the sections before and after the verse to understand where the verse fits. Often, prosperity preachers isolate a verse and use it out of context. Try to determine if the verse applies to a particular person or situation, or whether the verse is a universal promise.

The Bible contains many verses that declare God's blessings toward us and we should rejoice at this. God blesses us in order to meet our needs and enable us to give generously. The book of Proverbs teaches that hard, diligent work can lead to prosperity, but the prosperity gospel goes beyond these ideas and makes prosperity the goal of life. The prosperity gospel leads to idolatry: people worship God's blessings instead of God Himself.

Finally, in defense of the prosperity gospel, someone may say, *I've given money to prosperity gospel ministries and I've seen results.* If there has been a restoration of health or an improvement in someone's financial situation, it is appropriate to rejoice (see Rom. 12:15). Yet, to correlate sending money to a prosperity gospel ministry with God's blessing is faulty. Experiences must be judged by Scripture. Feelings and results cannot be the arbiter of truth. Just because something supposedly works does not mean that it is true. Christians have a responsibility to evaluate the means as well as the end. In other words, believers must discern if the end was reached in accordance with Scripture.

The goal of this book has been to inform readers about the prosperity gospel, including its history, theology, and errors, as well as to give biblical teaching on wealth, poverty, suffering, and giving. The prosperity gospel is a false gospel that contains false promises, promotes self-exaltation, and ultimately does not satisfy. It is our hope and prayer that the Lord will use this book to draw people away from the prosperity gospel and toward the gospel of Christ, for only in Him is there true prosperity.

For Further Study

For the reader interested in pursuing more in-depth study of the prosperity gospel movement, we suggest the following resources.

Alcorn, Randy. *Money, Possessions and Eternity.* Rev. ed. Wheaton, IL: Tyndale, 2003. Pp. 75–90.

Barron, Bruce. *The Health and Wealth Gospel: What's Going on Today in a Movement That Has Shaped the Faith of Millions.* Downers Grove, IL: InterVarsity, 1987.

Bowman Jr., Robert M. *The Word-Faith Controversy: Understanding the Health and Wealth Gospel.* Grand Rapids: Baker, 2001.

Fee, Gordon D. *The Disease of the Health and Wealth Gospels.* Vancouver, BC: Regent College Publishing, 1985.

Hanegraaff, Hank. *Christianity in Crisis: 21st Century.* Nashville: Thomas Nelson, 2009.

Horton, Michael. *Christless Christianity: The Alternative Gospel of the American Church.* Grand Rapids: Baker, 2008.

MacArthur Jr., John F. *Charismatic Chaos.* Grand Rapids: Zondervan, 1993. Pp. 322–53.

McConnell, D. R. *A Different Gospel.* Peabody, MA: Hendrickson, 1995.

Piper, John. *Let the Nations Be Glad! The Supremacy of God in Missions.* 3rd ed. Grand Rapids: Baker, 2010. Pp. 19–32.

Wilson-Hartgrove, Jonathan. *God's Economy: Redefining the Health and Wealth Gospel.* Grand Rapids: Zondervan, 2009.

Notes

PREFACE

1. David W. Jones, "The Bankruptcy of the Prosperity Gospel: An Exercise in Biblical and Theological Ethics," *Faith and Mission* 16, no. 1 (fall 1998): 79–87.
2. Eventually I wrote an article about the prosperity gospel and presented papers about financial topics at a couple of conferences. See Russell S. Woodbridge, "The Bankruptcy of Prosperity Theology: An Unprofitable Gospel," *Theology for Ministry* 3, no. 1 (May 2008): 5–26.

INTRODUCTION

1. Associated Press, "Believer Bitter over Prosperity Preachings" (Dec 27, 2007), available at http://www.religionnewsblog.com/20230/prosperity-gospel-4 (accessed July 20, 2010).
2. William Lobdell, "The Price of Healing," *LA Times*, July 27, 2003, available at http://www.trinityfi.org/press/latimes02.html (accessed November 3, 2008).
3. Ibid.
4. Tom Carter, comp., *2200 Quotations from the Writings of Charles H. Spurgeon* (Grand Rapids: Baker, 1988), 216.
5. Joel Osteen, *Your Best Life Now: 7 Steps to Living at Your Full Potential* (New York: FaithWords, 2004), 125.
6. Robert Tilton, *God's Word About Prosperity* (Dallas: Word of Faith Publications, 1983), 6.
7. Hanna Rosin, "Did Christianity Cause the Crash?" *The Atlantic*, December 2009, available at http://www.theatlantic.com/doc/200912/rosin-prosperity-gospel (accessed January 5, 2010).
8. See http://www.joelosteen.com and http://www.joycemeyer.org.
9. Pew Forum, *Spirit and Power: A 10-Country Survey of Pentecostals* (Washington, D.C.: Pew Research Center, 2006), 147.
10. Ibid., 147, 164.
11. Isaac Phiri and Joe Maxwell, "Gospel Riches," *Christianity Today* 51 (July 2007): 23.
12. Ibid., 24. Michael Okonkwo, a prosperity teacher in Nigeria and author of *Controlling Wealth God's Way*, claims that desiring to be wealthy is not a sin.
13. The ministries being investigated are those of Kenneth Copeland, Creflo Dollar, Benny Hinn, Eddie Long, Joyce Meyer, and Randy and Paula White.

14. Joel Osteen, *It's Your Time: Activate Your Faith, Achieve Your Dreams, and Increase in God's Favor* (New York: Free Press, 2009), 121, 123.

15. J. C. Ryle, *Knots Untied: Being Plain Statements on Disputed Points in Religion from the Standpoint of an Evangelical Churchman* (London: National Protestant Church Union, 1898), 19.

16. Millard J. Erickson, *Christian Theology* (Grand Rapids: Baker, 1985), 28.

CHAPTER 1: THE FOUNDATIONS OF THE PROSPERITY GOSPEL

1. Jerry Remy, with Corey Sandler, *Watching Baseball: Discovering the Game Within the Game*, 4th ed. (Guilford, CT: Lyons, 2008), 147.

2. See Art Lindsley, *C. S. Lewis's Case for Christ: Insights from Reason, Imagination and Faith* (Downers Grove, IL: InterVarsity Press, 2005), 43–44.

3. As Ecclesiastes 1:9 notes, there is nothing new under the sun. New Thought is an adaptation of the much earlier heresy known as Gnosticism and the Platonic belief that ideas depict true reality.

4. Charles H. Spurgeon, *The Salt-Cellars: Being a Collection of Proverbs, Together with Homely Notes Thereon* (New York: A. C. Armstrong, 1889), 18.

5. Horatio W. Dresser, *The Spirit of the New Thought: Essays and Addresses by Representative Authors and Leaders* (New York: Thomas Y. Crowell, 1917), vi.

6. William James, *The Varieties of Religious Experience* (London: Longmans, Green, and Co., 1905), 95.

7. For example, German philosophers Georg Hegel (1770–1831) and Arthur Schopenhauer (1788–1860) were proponents of German idealism. Idealism has many facets, but argues that reality depends upon ideas or the mind. Objects that we see in everyday life, such as apples, do not have properties, such as red and round, independent of our perception of them.

8. Martin A. Larson, *New Thought; or, a Modern Religious Approach: The Philosophy of Health, Happiness, and Prosperity* (New York: Philosophical Library, 1985), 6.

9. Charles S. Braden, *Spirits in Rebellion: The Rise and Development of New Thought* (Dallas: Southern Methodist University Press, 1963), 48–49.

10. Ibid., 54.

11. Phineas Quimby, *The Quimby Manuscripts*, 2nd ed., ed. Horatio Dresser (New York: Thomas Y. Crowell, 1921), 186.

12. Simon Coleman, *The Globalisation of Charismatic Christianity: Spreading the Gospel of Prosperity* (Cambridge: Cambridge University Press, 2000), 43.

13. Wallace D. Wattles, *The Science of Getting Rich* (Holyoke, MA: E. Towne, 1910), 9. Interestingly, the twenty-first century best-seller *The Secret* by Rhonda Byrne (New York: Atria, 2006) is merely an updated version of Wattles's heresy.

14. Sydney E. Ahlstrom, *A Religious History of the American People* (New Haven, CT: Yale University Press, 1972), 1030.

15. Braden, *Spirits in Rebellion*, 165.

16. Ibid.

17. Ralph Waldo Trine, *In Tune with the Infinite; or Fullness of Peace, Power and Plenty* (New York: Bobbs-Merrill, 1947), 206–7.

18. Ibid., 39.

19. Ibid., preface.

20. Braden, *Spirits in Rebellion*, 386–91.

21. Ibid., 387.

22. Norman Vincent Peale, *The Tough-Minded Optimist* (New York: Fireside, 2003), 29.

23. Ibid.

24. Ibid.

25. Unity beliefs available at http://www.unity.org/aboutunity/index.html (accessed April 23, 2009).

26. Emanuel Swedenborg, *Divine Providence* (New York: Swedenborg Foundation, 1949), 3.

27. Larson, *New Thought*, 23.

28. Ernest Holmes, *Creative Mind and Success* (New York: Robert M. McBride, 1919), 4.

29. Trine, *In Tune with the Infinite*, 11.

30. Jennie H. Croft, "Answers to Questions in Unity" (Unity Tract Society), 394.

31. Wattles, *Science of Getting Rich*, 1.

32. Larson, *New Thought*, 27.

33. Ibid.

34. Charles Fillmore, *Prosperity* (Unity Village, MO: Unity Books, 1936), 1.

35. Ibid., 2.

36. Ibid., 1.

37. Trine, *In Tune with the Infinite*, 180.

38. Principles of International New Thought Alliance available at http://www.newthoughtalliance.org/about.htm (accessed August 4, 2010).

39. Napoleon Hill, *Success Through a Positive Mental Attitude* (Englewood Cliffs, NJ: Prentice-Hall, 1960), 59.

40. Napoleon Hill, *Think and Grow Rich* (Meriden, CT: Ralston Society, 1938), 253.

41. Trine, *In Tune with the Infinite*, 179.

42. Ibid., 176–77.

43. Holmes, *Creative Mind and Success*, 20.

44. Charles Haanel, *The Master Key System* (New York: Penguin, 2007), 114.

45. Principles of International New Thought Alliance available at http://www.newthoughtalliance.org/about.htm (accessed January 24, 2008).

46. Trine, *In Tune with the Infinite*, 16, 18.

47. Ibid., 13.

48. "Declaration of Principles," International New Thought Alliance, available at http://www.newthoughtalliance.org/about.htm (accessed January 24, 2008).

49. Holmes, *Creative Mind and Success*, 13.

50. Warren Evans, *The Mental Cure* (Boston: Colby and Rich, 1886), 22–23.

51. Holmes, *Creative Mind and Success*, 19, 21.

52. Trine, *In Tune with the Infinite*, 42.

53. Ibid., 84.

54. Quimby, *Quimby Manuscripts*, 175.

55. Thomas Troward, *The Law and the Word* (New York: Robert M. McBride, 1920), 93.

56. Henry Hamblin, *Dynamic Thought* (Chicago: Personality Institute, 1923), 130.

57. Larson, *New Thought*, 38.

58. Wattles, *Science of Getting Rich*, 9.

59. Hill, *Think and Grow Rich*, 49.

60. Ibid., 71.

61. Robert Collier, *Secret of the Ages* (New York: Robert Collier, 1926), 107.

62. Holmes, *Creative Mind and Success*, 48.

63. Wattles, *Science of Getting Rich*, 75.

64. Emanuel Swedenborg, *The Apocalypse Explained*, vol. 5, 12th ed. (New York: Swedenborg Foundation, 1982), 117. See also page 6 for a rejection of Jesus' work on the cross.

65. International New Thought Alliance Web site, http://www.newthoughtalliance.org/about.htm (accessed May 1, 2009).

66. Trine, *In Tune with the Infinite*, 203–11.

67. Nathan R. Wood, *The Secret of the Universe* (New York: F. H. Revell, 1932), 66.

CHAPTER 2: THE TEACHINGS OF THE PROSPERITY GOSPEL

1. Milmon F. Harrison, *Righteous Riches: The Word of Faith Movement in Contemporary African American Religion* (Oxford: Oxford University Press, 2005), 6.

2. D. R. McConnell, *A Different Gospel: A Historical and Biblical Analysis of the Modern Faith Movement* (Peabody, MA: Hendrickson, 1988), 45. McConnell provides convincing evidence of Kenyon's syncretism and the influence of metaphysics. Kenyon writes, "The Lord Jesus was not, however, a 'one-of-a-kind.' 'Incarnation' can be repeated in each and every one of us. Every man who has been 'born again' is an Incarnation." He also writes, "The believer is as much of an Incarnation as was Jesus of Nazareth." E. W. Kenyon, *The Father and His Family* (Lynwood, WA: Kenyon's Gospel Publishing Society, 1981), 100, 118.

3. Dale H. Simmons, *E. W. Kenyon and the Postbellum Pursuit of Peace, Power, and Plenty* (Lanham, MD: Scarecrow Press, 1997), xi.

4. Harrison, *Righteous Riches*, 6. The idea that the mind creates reality emerges in its principal form from philosophical Idealism, a position held by German philosopher Georg Hegel (1770–1831).

5. E. W. Kenyon, *Jesus the Healer* (Seattle: Kenyon's Gospel Publishing Society, 1943), 26, as quoted in Michael G. Moriarty, *The New Charismatics: A Concerned Voice Responds to Dangerous New Trends* (Grand Rapids: Zondervan, 1992), 79.

6. As quoted in Simmons, *E. W. Kenyon*, 172.

7. E. W. Kenyon, *Advanced Bible Course: Studies in the Deeper Life* (Lynnwood, WA: Kenyon's Gospel Publishing Society, 1970), 279.

8. E. W. Kenyon, *What Happened from the Cross to the Throne*, 5th ed. (Lynnwood, WA: Kenyon's Gospel Publishing Society, 1969), 47.

9. As quoted in Simmons, *E. W. Kenyon*, 235.

10. Ibid., 246. Ironically, though Kenyon believed that with God you could never make a bad investment, Kenyon lost all of his money in a poor investment in the oil business.

11. McConnell, *A Different Gospel*, 25.

12. From Kenneth Hagin Ministries Web site, http://www.rhema.org/index.php?option =com_content&view=article&id=18&Itemid=36 (accessed April 30, 2009).

13. McConnell, *A Different Gospel*, 57–76.

14. Kenneth E. Hagin, *How to Write Your Own Ticket with God* (Tulsa: Kenneth Hagin Ministries, 1979), 6–8.

15. McConnell, *A Different Gospel*, 6–12.

16. Ibid., 63.

17. Harrison, *Righteous Riches*, 14–17. In 1979, Doyle Harrison founded the International Convention of Faith Ministries to minister to those who are called to hold forth, contend for, and propagate the Word of Faith worldwide. In 1985, Kenneth Hagin Sr. started the Rhema Ministerial Association International, an organization that licenses and ordains graduates and equips ministers. Five years later, the Fellowship of Inner-City Word of Faith started and today has approximately three hundred members.

18. For example, see John MacArthur, *Charismatic Chaos* (Grand Rapids: Zondervan, 1992); Hank Hanegraaff, *Christianity in Crisis* (Eugene, OR: Harvest House, 1993); Michael Horton, ed., *The Agony of Deceit* (Chicago: Moody, 1990); Dave Hunt and T. A. McMahon, *The Seduction of Christianity: Spiritual Discernment in the Last Days* (Eugene, OR: Harvest House, 1985).

19. See their belief statement at http://www.thepottershouse.org/Local/About-Us/Belief -Statement.aspx (accessed January 23, 2008).

20. See Jerry L. Buckner, "Concerns About the Teachings of T. D. Jakes: The Man, His Ministry, and His Movement," *Christian Research Journal*, 22, no. 2 (1999), http:// www.equip.org/site/c.muI1LaMNJrE/b.2625875/k.B807/DJ900.htm (accessed January 23, 2008), http://www.equip.org/articles/concerns-about-the-teachings-of-t-d -jakes.

21. Ibid.

22. Hanegraaff, *Christianity in Crisis*, 123–24.

23. See "We Believe" at http://www.bennyhinn.org/aboutus/articledesc.cfm?id=1392 (accessed August 15, 2009).

24. See "Statement of Beliefs" at http://www.worldchangers.org/Statement-Of-Beliefs. aspx (accessed August 14, 2009).

25. Kenneth Copeland, *Praise-a-Thon* program on TBN (April 1988), as quoted in Hanegraaff, *Christianity in Crisis*, 125. Copeland was suggesting that God has been disappointed or suffered setbacks just like us and we get down on ourselves. His

fuller quotation is, "I mean, He lost His top-ranking, most anointed angel; the first man He ever created; the first woman He ever created; the whole earth and all the Fullness therein; a third of the angels, at least—that's a big loss, man." Arguably, Copeland was trying to encourage his audience, but instead he ends up demeaning God's character and sovereignty.

26. Charles Capps, *The Tongue, A Creative Force* (Tulsa: Harrison House, 1976), 117–18.

27. Creflo Dollar, "Faith: The Power That Brings the World to Its Knees: Calling Those Things That Be Not as Though They Were," June 2, 2009, http://www.creflodollarministries.org/BibleStudy/StudyNotes.aspx?id=786 (accessed August 27, 2009).

28. Ibid.

29. Kenneth Copeland, *The Laws of Prosperity* (Fort Worth: Kenneth Copeland Publications, 1974), 98.

30. Kenneth Copeland, "Applying Faith in Prayer," June 9, 2009, http://kenneth-copeland-ministries.com/98/applying-faith-in-prayer-by-kenneth-copeland/ (accessed August 27, 2009).

31. Ibid.

32. Joyce Meyer, "List of Confessions," http://www.joycemeyer.org/OurMinistries/Everyday Answers/FeaturedHandouts/listofconfessionsbyjoycemeyer.htm (accessed August 23, 2009).

33. Joel Osteen, *Your Best Life Now* (New York: Faith Words, 2004), 109.

34. Ibid., 122.

35. Ibid., 38–39.

36. Paul Crouch on *Praise the Lord* on TBN July 7, 1986.

37. Kenneth Copeland, "The Force of Love" (Fort Worth: Kenneth Copeland Ministries, 1987), audiotape #02-0028, as quoted in Hanegraaff, *Christianity in Crisis*, 186.

38. Another interpretation of this verse is that it refers to the divine council—the "gods" or spirit beings appointed by God over the nations. Whether it refers to corrupt judges or the divine council, it certainly does not make humans into gods.

39. In editing this work, the authors were unable to reverify Dollar's claim, since, curiously, the transcripts for most of his messages from 2001 and 2002 have been removed from his ministry Web site.

40. T. D. Jakes, "MegaCare, 1," *The Potter's Touch*, iTunes Podcast, Lightsource.com, August 17, 2008.

41. Martin C. Evans, "Gospel: Bringing in the Cash," *Newsday*, November 11, 2006, http://www.newsday.com/news/local/newyork/ny-lidoll1112,0,5446471.story?coll=ny-top-headlines (accessed January 23, 2008).

42. Libby Copeland, "With Gifts from God," *Washington Post*, March 25, 2001, http://www.trinityfi.org/press/tdjakes01.html (accessed January 25, 2008).

43. Robert Tilton, *Success in Life*, program on TBN, December 27, 1990, quoted in Hanegraaff, *Christianity in Crisis*, 186.

44. Copeland, *Laws of Prosperity*, 26.

45. Gloria Copeland, *God's Will Is Prosperity* (Fort Worth: Kenneth Copeland Publications, 1996), 45.

46. Theologian Ken Sarles rightly noted that "the Law of Compensation [is] the bedrock of the prosperity movement." Ken L. Sarles, "A Theological Evaluation of the Prosperity Gospel," *Bibliotheca Sacra* 143 (Oct.–Dec. 1986): 349.

47. Gloria Copeland, *God's Will Is Prosperity*, 54.

48. Edward Pousson, *Spreading the Flame* (Grand Rapids: Zondervan, 1992), 159.

49. Kenneth Copeland, *Laws of Prosperity*, 51.

50. Paula White, "Prosperity," http://www.paulawhite.org/blog/comments/prosperity (accessed September 3, 2009).

51. Creflo Dollar, "The Origin of Prosperity," May 11, 2003, http://www.creflodollar ministries.org/BibleStudy/StudyNotes.aspx?id=432 (accessed August, 27, 2009).

52. Laurie Goodstein, "Believers Invest in the Gospel of Getting Rich," *New York Times*, August 16, 2009, A1.

53. Ibid.

54. Carolyn Tuft and Bill Smith, "Full Story: From Fenton to Fortune in the Name of God," *St. Louis Post-Dispatch*, November 13, 2003, http://www.stltoday.com/stltoday /news/special/joycemeyer.nsf/0/C5099399D2FCC5FA86256DDF00661C5F?Open Document (accessed September 3, 2009).

55. The ministries are those of Kenneth Copeland, Creflo Dollar, Benny Hinn, Eddie Long, Joyce Meyer, and Randy and Paula White. Many of these leaders are known for their exorbitant lifestyles.

56. Kenneth Hagin, "Healing: The Father's Provision," *Word of Faith*, August 1977, 9, as quoted in D. R. McConnell, *A Different Gospel*, updated ed. (Peabody, MA: Hendrickson, 1995), 146.

57. Robert Bolden, "A Look at Asthma," *Ever Increasing Faith* 5, no. 2 (summer 2009): 17.

58. Joyce Meyer, "Healing Scriptures," http://www.joycemeyer.org/OurMinistries/Every dayAnswers/FeaturedHandouts/healingscriptures (accessed August 4, 2010).

59. Ibid.

60. World Changers International, "Statement of Beliefs," http://www.worldchangers. org/Statement-Of-Beliefs.aspx (accessed November 29, 2009).

61. Joyce Meyer, "Statement of Faith," http://www.joycemeyer.org/AboutUs/Statement OfFaith (accessed November 29, 2009).

62. Kenneth Copeland, "Question & Answer," *Believer's Voice of Victory* (August 1988).

63. Ibid.

64. Creflo Dollar, "Jesus' Growth into Sonship" (*Creflo Dollar Ministries, World Changers* broadcast, December 8, 2002). For more information about Dollar's beliefs about humanity, see Let Us Reason Ministries, "Creflo Dollar Teaching on the God/man," available at www.letusreason.org/poptea16.htm (accessed June 5, 2009).

65. As quoted in Hanegraaff, *Christianity in Crisis*, 164.

66. As quoted in McConnell, *A Different Gospel*, 120.

67. See Wayne Grudem, "He Did Not Descend into Hell: A Plea for Following Scripture Instead of the Apostle's Creed," *Journal of the Evangelical Society* 34, no. 1 (March 1991): 103–13.

68. Gordon Fee, "The Cult of Prosperity," *Reformation Today* 82 (Nov.–Dec. 1984): 13.

69. Osteen, *Your Best Life Now*, 143–52.

70. Ibid.

71. Ibid., 149.

72. See D. A. Carson, *The Gospel According to John* (Grand Rapids: Eerdmans, 1991), 244.

73. Joel Osteen, *Become a Better You* (New York: Free Press, 2007), 129.

74. Joel Osteen, *It's Your Time: Activate Your Faith, Achieve Your Dreams, and Increase in God's Favor* (New York: Free Press, 2009), 173.

75. Osteen, *Your Best Life Now*, 125.

76. Ibid., 130.

77. Ibid., 114.

78. Ibid., 131.

79. Ibid., 130.

80. Osteen, *It's Your Time*, 47, 121, 123.

81. Osteen, *Your Best Life Now*, 310. This invitation is after the footnotes. He expands the presentation slightly in *Become a Better You*.

82. Osteen, *Become a Better You*, 129–30. Emphasis added.

83. Osteen, *It's Your Time*, 52.

84. Osteen, *Become a Better You*, 89.

85. Ibid., 91.

86. Ibid., 35.

87. Ibid., 61.

88. Ibid., 43.

89. Ibid., 45.

90. Ibid., 69.

91. "Joel Osteen Answers His Critics," *60 Minutes*, CBS, aired October 14, 2007. Transcript (dated December 23, 2007) available at http://www.cbsnews.com/stories/2007/10/11/60minutes/main3358652.shtml (accessed February 1, 2008).

92. Interview with Joel Osteen, *Larry King Live*, CNN, aired June 20, 2005. Transcript available at http://transcripts.cnn.com/TRANSCRIPTS/0506/20/lkl.01.html (accessed February 1, 2008).

93. Ibid.

94. Interview with Joel Osteen, *Fox News Sunday with Chris Wallace*, aired December 23, 2007. Partial transcript available at http://www.foxnews.com/story/0,2933,318054,00.html (accessed January 30, 2008).

CHAPTER 3: THE ERRORS OF THE PROSPERITY GOSPEL

1. C. J. Mahaney, *The Cross Centered Life: Keeping the Gospel the Main Thing* (Sisters, OR: Multnomah, 2002), 20–21.

2. Charles Spurgeon, *Spurgeon at His Best* (Grand Rapids: Baker, 1988), 17. This quotation is from Spurgeon's sermon entitled, "The Heart of the Gospel," delivered on July 18, 1886.

3. J. C. Ryle, *Living or Dead? A Series of Home Truths* (New York: Robert Carter, 1852), 121.

4. Jerry Bridges, "Gospel-Driven Sanctification," *Modern Reformation Magazine* 12, no. 3 (May/June 2003): 14.

5. Byron Pitts, "Joel Osteen Answers His Critics," *60 Minutes*, CBS, aired October 14, 2007. Transcript (dated December 23, 2007) available at http://www.cbsnews.com /stories/2007/10/11/60minutes/main3358652.shtml (accessed February 1, 2008).

6. Ibid.

7. Michael S. Horton, "Whatever Happened to Sin?" http://www.wscal.edu/faculty /wscwritings/horton.osteen (accessed September 24, 2009).

8. J. D. Douglas and Merrill C. Tenny, eds., *The New International Dictionary of the Bible* (Grand Rapids: Zondervan, 1987), s.v. "faith."

9. Kenneth Copeland, *The Laws of Prosperity* (Fort Worth: Kenneth Copeland Publications, 1974), 19.

10. Ibid., 41.

11. Joel Osteen, *Become a Better You* (New York: Free Press, 2007), 131.

12. Kenneth E. Hagin, *Having Faith in Your Faith* (Tulsa: Kenneth Hagin Ministries, 1988), 4.

13. Joyce Meyer, *Approval Addiction: Overcoming Your Need to Please Everyone* (New York: Faith Words, 2005), 9–10. See Hank Hanegraaff, *Christianity in Crisis: The 21st Century* (Nashville: Thomas Nelson, 2009), 123–28.

14. Ken L. Sarles, "A Theological Evaluation of the Prosperity Gospel," *Bibliotheca Sacra* 143 (Oct.–Dec. 1986): 339.

15. Kenneth Copeland, *The Troublemaker* (Fort Worth: Kenneth Copeland Publications, 1996), 6.

16. John Avanzini, *Believer's Voice of Victory*, program on TBN, January 20, 1991. Quoted in Hanegraaff, *Christianity in Crisis*, 381.

17. John Avanzini, *Praise the Lord*, program on TBN, September 15, 1988. Quoted in Hanegraaff, *Christianity in Crisis*, 381.

18. John Avanzini, *Believer's Voice of Victory*, program on TBN, January 20, 1991. Quoted in Hanegraaff, *Christianity in Crisis*, 381.

19. Joyce Meyer, *Healing Scriptures* (Fenton, MO: Joyce Meyer Ministries, 2008), 26.

20. Kenneth E. Hagin, *Redeemed from Poverty, Sickness, and Spiritual Death* (Tulsa: Faith Library, 1983), 16.

21. Meyer, *Healing Scriptures*, 14–15.

22. Robert Tilton, *God's Laws of Success* (Dallas: Word of Faith Publications, 1983), 71.

23. Some prosperity teachers may object to this interpretation because Matthew 8:16–17 mentions that Jesus healed all who were sick in fulfillment of Isaiah's prophecy. In his gospel, however, Matthew is not making a case for guaranteed, physical healing

for today in the atonement. Rather he is pointing to Jesus' healing ministry that supported His messianic claims. It is the case that the Hebrew prophets looked forward to a day of healing when the peace of God restored creation in its entirety. But this is not yet reality, a perspective missing among prosperity thinkers.

24. Hanegraaff, *Christianity in Crisis*, 256.

25. This important covenant is mentioned numerous times in the writings of the prosperity teachers, i.e., Gloria Copeland, *God's Will Is Prosperity* (Fort Worth: Kenneth Copeland Publications, 1973), 4–6; Kenneth Copeland, *Laws of Prosperity*, 51; Kenneth Copeland, *Our Covenant with God* (Fort Worth: Kenneth Copeland Publications, 1987), 10; and Kenneth Copeland, *The Troublemaker*, 6.

26. Prosperity teacher Kenneth Copeland articulated the movement's view of the inception of the Abrahamic covenant best when he wrote that "after Adam's fall in the Garden, God needed an avenue back into the earth. . . . Since man was the key figure in the Fall, man had to be the key figure in the redemption, so God approached a man named Abram. He reenacted with Abram what Satan had done with Adam. . . . God offered Abram a proposition and Abram bought it." Kenneth Copeland, *Our Covenant with God*, 10.

27. Edward Pousson, *Spreading the Flame: Charismatic Churches and Missions Today* (Grand Rapids: Zondervan, 1992), 158.

28. Paula White, "Covenant," July 15, 2009, available at www.paulawhite.org/blog /comments/covenant (accessed October 1, 2009).

29. Kenneth Copeland, *Laws of Prosperity*, 51.

30. Creflo Dollar, "The Foundation of Covenant," sermon notes, May 25, 2003, http://www.creflodollarministries.org/BibleStudy/StudyNotes.aspx?id=433 (accessed October 4, 2009).

31. Osteen, *Become a Better You*, 40.

32. Harvey Cox, *Fire from Heaven* (Reading, MA: Addison-Wesley, 1995), 271.

33. That the Abrahamic covenant is an unconditional covenant can be demonstrated by four facts. First, the covenant ceremony in Genesis 15 was unilateral. In fact, Abraham was asleep. Second, no conditions are stated in the covenant. Third, in the restatement of the covenant in Genesis 17:7, 13, and 19, the covenant is called "everlasting." Finally, the covenant was confirmed despite Abraham's continued disobedience and lack of faith.

34. There is some debate among theologians as to the possibility that some biblical covenants may be dissoluble. For example, some identify the Mosaic covenant as being dissolvable on account of the conditions that were attached to it (see Exod. 19–24; 34:27; Deut. 11:26–28). For more information on the topic, see: David W. Jones and John K. Tarwater, "Are Biblical Covenants Dissolvable? Toward a Theology of Marriage," *Southwestern Journal of Theology* 47, no. 1 (fall 2004): 1–11; and Bruce K. Waltke, "The Phenomenon of Conditionality Within Unconditional Covenants," in *Israel's Apostasy and Restoration: Essays in Honor of Roland K. Harrison*, ed. Avraham Gileadi (Grand Rapids: Zondervan, 1988), 123–39.

35. Duane A. Garrett, *Proverbs, Ecclesiastes, Song of Songs*, The New American Commentary, vol. 14 (Nashville: Broadman & Holman, 1993), 167.

36. Creflo Dollar, "Prayer: Your Path to Success," March 2, 2009, http://www.creflo dollarministries.org/BibleStudy/Articles.aspx?id=329 (accessed on October 8, 2009).

37. Creflo Dollar, "Pray by the Rules," March 9, 2009, http://www.creflodollar ministries.org/BibleStudy/Articles.aspx?id=330 (accessed on October 8, 2009).

38. John MacArthur, *Alone with God* (Wheaton, IL: Victor Books, 1995), 51.

39. Sarles, "Theological Evaluation," 337.

40. Sarles says that this is an "often quoted verse" in the prosperity movement ("Theological Evaluation," 338). Hanegraaff wrote that 3 John 2 was a "classic example" of prosperity misinterpretation (*Christianity in Crisis*, 223). Gordon Fee called 3 John 2 "the basic Scripture text of the cult of prosperity" ("The 'Gospel' of Prosperity," *Reformation Today* 82 [Nov.–Dec., 1984]: 40). Bruce Barron wrote that 3 John 2 was "the 'Old Faithful' of prosperity proof texts" (*The Health and Wealth Gospel: What's Going on Today in a Movement That Has Shaped the Faith of Millions?* [Downers Grove, IL: InterVarsity Press, 1987], 91).

41. For a full account of Roberts's miraculous revelation concerning 3 John 2, see Barron, *Health and Wealth Gospel*, 62.

42. Kenneth S. Kantzer, "The Cut-Rate Grace of a Health and Wealth Gospel," *Christianity Today* 29 (June 1985): 14.

43. Barron, *Health and Wealth Gospel*, 91.

44. Joseph Henry Thayer, *The New Thayer's Greek-English Lexicon of the New Testament* (Peabody, MA: Hendrickson, 1981), 260.

45. Gloria Copeland, *God's Will Is Prosperity*, 54.

46. Shayne Lee, *T. D. Jakes: America's New Preacher* (New York: New York University, 2005), 110–11.

47. James R. Goff Jr., "The Faith That Claims," *Christianity Today* 34 (February 1990): 21.

CHAPTER 4: THE BIBLICAL TEACHING ON SUFFERING

1. Note that James likewise identified "the purpose of the Lord" in Job's suffering as the provision of an occasion on which to demonstrate that "the Lord is compassionate and merciful" (James 5:11).

2. Christopher W. Morgan and Robert A. Peterson, eds., *Suffering and the Goodness of God* (Wheaton, IL: Crossway, 2008), 142.

3. As theologians have debated free will, two general positions have emerged. Some have espoused the idea of a so-called "volitional free will," which is the understanding that people are free to choose from the available options. Others have adopted a wider view, holding a so-called "libertarian free will" or a "contra-causal free will." This is the idea that humanity's will is completely free—that is, free to choose any option. Of course, there are a myriad of hybrid views and other options. For more information on this topic, especially as it relates to salvation, see: R. C. Sproul, *Willing to Believe: The Controversy over Free Will* (Grand Rapids: Baker, 2002); David

Basinger, ed., *Predestination and Free Will: Four Views of Divine Sovereignty and Human Freedom* (Downers Grove, IL: InterVarsity Press, 1985); and Robert Kane, *A Contemporary Introduction to Free Will* (New York: Oxford University Press, 2005).

4. Morgan and Peterson, eds., *Suffering and the Goodness of God*, 85.

CHAPTER 5: THE BIBLICAL TEACHING ON WEALTH AND POVERTY

1. Jesus warned His followers, "Beware of false prophets, who come to you in sheep's clothing but inwardly are ravenous wolves" (Matt. 7:15). Note that sheep's clothing was the dress of prophets (see Heb. 11:37).

2. Christian Stewardship Association, "Dollars and Percents," *Stewardship Matters* 2, no. 1 (1998): 11.

3. Interestingly, Matthew's account of the Beatitudes specifies, "Blessed are the poor *in spirit*, for theirs is the kingdom of heaven" (5:3 emphasis added). Yet, Luke's "Blessed are you who are poor, for yours is the kingdom of God" (6:20) is surely economic in nature, as his complementary woe communicates, "But woe to you who are rich, for you have received your consolation" (6:24).

4. Perhaps the fact that humans have material needs is one of the ways in which they were made "a little less than God" (Pss. 8:5 HCSB), for God is a Spirit (see John 4:24), who has no material needs (see Pss. 50:10–12; 121:4; Hag. 2:8). Note, however, that Jesus currently does possess a resurrection body (see Luke 24:39), the same body that believers will one day receive (see Rom. 8:11; Phil. 3:21; 1 John 3:2). Additionally, while it would surely be incorrect to label it as a need, it is interesting to note that Jesus purposely ate in His resurrection body as a demonstration of its material nature (see Luke 24:41–42).

5. A related error is to assume that the material world is inferior to the spiritual world. This type of Platonic thought not only degrades the good nature of the physical world that God made (see Gen. 1:4, 10, 12, 18, 21, 25, 31; 2:9, 12) but also overlooks the fact that believers' everlasting home will be the present physical world made new (see Acts 3:21; Rom. 8:18–22; Rev. 21:1–22:5).

6. Interestingly, Adam seems to have been the one who was primarily entrusted with the duty to work (in a formal sense, see Gen. 2:15, 19–20; 3:17–19), while Eve was charged with childbearing (see Gen. 3:16). In so doing, each were functionally bearing God's image as the Lord Himself is both a worker and a creator, respectively. Furthermore, neither Adam nor Eve could effectively accomplish their divinely assigned duty apart from the assistance of the other.

7. There is some debate regarding the diet of Adam and Eve in the garden of Eden. While it is true that there is no record of humankind being given permission to eat the meat of animals until after the flood (see Gen. 9:3), there is simply not enough information in Scripture to be dogmatic on the issue. In any event, contemporary people have been given the meat of animals to eat; thus, no one should call this practice unclean (see Acts 10:15).

8. Note that despite being commanded to procreate (see Gen. 1:28), Adam and Eve had no children until after the fall of man (see Gen. 4:1); it can be deduced that their stay in the garden of Eden was quite brief.

9. Interestingly, since people are made in God's image, and since the work assigned to them involved functionally bearing God's image, engaging in such labor is ultimately fulfilling. This is true for both women (see 1 Tim. 2:15) and men (see Eph. 4:28; 1 Thess. 4:11–12; 2 Thess. 3:7–13; 1 Tim. 5:8).

10. It should be noted that the notion of a "preferential option for the poor," popular in many theologically moderate twentieth-century writings (see Richard John Neuhaus, ed., *The Preferential Option for the Poor* [Grand Rapids: Eerdmans, 1988]), is largely incorrect in its analysis and claims; biblically speaking, the divine "preference" for poverty is one of circumstances, not of persons.

11. For more information on the civil law as being a static manifestation of the moral law, see Walter Kaiser, *Toward Rediscovering the Old Testament* (Grand Rapids: Zondervan, 1991), 163; and Walter Kaiser, *Toward Old Testament Ethics* (Grand Rapids: Zondervan, 1983), 81–137.

12. As Scripture does not record the specific observance of the Sabbath Year, there is much debate among scholars as to whether or not it was ever actually observed by the Jews. Second Chronicles 36:21 indicates that the length of the Babylonian captivity was in order to make up for the Jews' neglect of the Sabbath Year. This would have been in accord with the warning given by God in Leviticus 26:34–35. Since the Babylonian captivity was seventy years in length (see Jer. 25:12; 29:10), this would account for 490 years of neglected observance. Note that 1 Maccabees 6:49 does seem to indicate observance of the Sabbath Year at a time during the intertestamental period.

13. Note that the economic law stipulated that lands owned by the Levites could not be sold. This is likely because, as priests, the Levites most clearly represented the Lord, who is the true eternal owner of all the land (see Ps. 24:1–2, "The earth is the Lord's and the fullness thereof, the world and those who dwell therein, for he has founded it upon the seas and established it upon the rivers").

14. Resting, as well as laboring, is part of bearing God's image (see Eccl. 2:24–26), for the Lord Himself rested (see Gen. 2:1–4). Note, as well, that God's rest, not the creation of humanity, is the apex of the creation week.

15. Foreigners, however, did not have to be released (see Lev. 25:44–46). This is likely because the Year of Jubilee foreshadowed redemption, and unbelievers are not redeemed.

16. There were, of course, numerous other non-Sabbath-related economic laws and principles, the majority of which seem to likewise be crafted in order to protect the poor. Examples of such regulations include commands not to mistreat the poor and to be generous (see Exod. 22:21; 23:9; Lev. 19:33–34; Deut. 10:19), the rights of a kinsman-redeemer to rescue a financially distressed family member (see Lev. 25:25), food for the poor and needy (see Deut. 14:28–29; 26:12–15), a

sliding scale of sacrificial offerings (see Lev. 5:7, 11; 12:8; 14:21–22), and a ban on taking another's livelihood as collateral for a loan (see Exod. 22:26; Deut. 24:6, 12–13), among others.

17. One of the possible reasons for this is that walled towns communicated security and were symbolic of the New Jerusalem (see Rev. 21:2–14); thus, home sales within walled towns were permanent (i.e., eternal).

18. John Frame, *The Doctrine of the Christian Life: A Theology of Lordship* (Philipsburg, NJ: P&R, 2008), 824.

19. Prior to the institution of the monarchy, the only formal tax that was required of the Jews was the temple/tabernacle tax (unless one considers the various tithes to be a tax). The temple/tabernacle tax was used to meet the everyday operating expenses of the Jewish place of worship. In Exodus 30:11–16 Moses set this tax at a half shekel for every male over the age of twenty. Roughly seven hundred years after Moses' time, Joash reinstated this tax (see 2 Chron. 24:6–10). Then, about three hundred years after the time of Joash, Nehemiah imposed this tax, setting it at a third of a shekel (see Neh. 10:32). In Jesus' time, approximately 425 years after the time of Nehemiah, the tax was again observed as a half-shekel tax (see Matt. 17:24–27).

20. See also Proverbs 12:11, 27; 14:23.

21. See also Proverbs 13:4; 20:4.

22. John Stott, *Issues Facing Christians Today*, 4th ed. (Grand Rapids: InterVarsity Press, 2006), 3–5. As examples of Psalms that mention the Lord saving the poor from the wicked, Stott cites Psalms 22, 25, 37, 40, 69, 74, and 149.

23. Leviticus 12:8, "And if she cannot afford a lamb, then she shall take two turtledoves or two pigeons, one for a burnt offering and the other for a sin offering. And the priest shall make atonement for her, and she shall be clean" (see Exod. 13:2, 12–15).

24. Jesus' material needs, as well as those of His disciples, were apparently met by women who followed Him and were part of His ministry (see Luke 10:38–42; John 12:1–11). This simple lifestyle freed Jesus and His disciples from many of the cares that accompany fiscal management. Such an arrangement may have been necessary given the short tenure of Christ's earthly ministry.

25. Another way to look at Jesus' poverty would be to consider the spiritual poverty inherent to His incarnation. For example, verses that could be appealed to include 2 Corinthians 8:9, "For you know the grace of our Lord Jesus Christ, that though he was rich, yet for your sake he became poor, so that you by his poverty might become rich," and Philippians 2:6–7, "Though he was in the form of God, did not count equality with God a thing to be grasped, but made himself nothing, taking the form of a servant, being born in the likeness of men."

26. Interestingly, upon his salvation, Zacchaeus promised to give only *half* of his goods to the poor, yet was lauded for his willingness to do so (see Luke 19:8–9). This is in contrast to other disciples who gave up all to follow Christ (see Mark 1:18; 10:28; Luke 14:33).

27. Contextually, note that in His reference to material increase in Mark 10:29–30, Jesus was speaking about life on the new earth.

28. The duty to work in order to meet material needs was assumed in the New Testament era. Indeed, with the end of the Old Testament theocracy and being under Roman rule, there was no other way for able-bodied Jewish people to secure income. Additionally, note the way in which beggars and begging are described in the Gospels and in the book of Acts (see Mark 10:46–48; Luke 16:3, 20–21; John 9:6; Acts 3:2). See also Matthew 20:1–15 and Luke 10:7, which endorse labor.

29. In accord with the message of Proverbs 17:5 and 19:17, Jesus explained to His followers, "I was thirsty and you gave me drink, I was a stranger and you welcomed me, I was naked and you clothed me, I was sick and you visited me, I was in prison and you came to me" (Matt. 25:35–36). The picture here seems to be of the cross where Jesus was thirsty, alone, naked, sick, and in prison. Christ's message, then, is that the cross will prompt His followers to treat others in accord with their faith in Him.

30. Jesus' statement, "For you always have the poor with you" (Mark 14:7), which is a citation of Deuteronomy 15:11, was not intended to be an excuse for complacency but rather was a motivator to act (see Deut. 15:4).

31. It is easy to overlook the fact that the rich, young ruler was not only putting his faith in his money but also in his position of authority (note that only Luke informs his readers that the man was a "ruler" [18:18]). This is evident in that Jesus did not simply instruct the man to divest himself of his wealth, but rather, as all three Synoptic Gospel writers explicitly report, Christ commanded the man to give his money to *the poor*—that is, to the powerless (see Matt. 19:21; Mark 10:21; Luke 18:22). For a similar teaching, see Jesus' parable of the rich fool (see Luke 12:13–21).

32. While Jesus' disciples were being trained in the essentials of ministry, Christ had prohibited them from taking many material goods on their travels (see Luke 9:3; 10:4). However, once trained, and in light of Jesus' imminent departure, in Luke 22:35–36 He instructed them to wisely use material goods to facilitate their ministry.

33. See also Acts 18:3; 1 Corinthians 4:12; 9:3–14; 1 Thessalonians 2:9; 2 Thessalonians 3:7–9.

34. Some have gone beyond positing Acts 2:44–45 and 4:32–35 as being normative for the Christian life to suggesting that this passage supports Marxist communism. In addition to the problems cited in the text concerning the application of Acts 2:44–45 and 4:32–35 to the modern church, note the following distinctions between the communal living example in Acts and Marxist communism: it was spontaneous, not planned; it was voluntary, not coerced; it was private, not government controlled; it was a blessing, not an entitlement; it involved personal relationships, not sterile bureaucracy; it was driven by the love of the wealthy, not the envy of the poor; and it was sustained by private property, it did not eliminate private property.

35. See also Romans 1:29; 1 Corinthians 5:11; 6:10; Ephesians 5:3; Colossians 3:5; James 4:2; 2 Peter 2:14.

36. Most Christians recognize covetousness as a sin, in light of its articulation in the Ten Commandments. Yet, interestingly, the spiritual stumbling block of coveting does not receive as much attention in the modern church as some of the other sins prohibited in the Decalogue. This is surprising given the frequency with which coveting is cited in the New Testament. Note that Paul revealed that awareness of his own covetous nature was one of the factors that drew him to Christ (see Rom. 7:7). Moreover, Paul was careful to remind his readers that covetousness was not present in his own ministry (see Acts 20:33; 1 Thess. 2:5).

CHAPTER 6: THE BIBLICAL TEACHING ON GIVING

1. Dietrich Bonhoeffer, *The Cost of Discipleship* (London: SCM Press, 2001), 120–21.
2. John Calvin, *Commentary on a Harmony of the Evangelists*, vol. 1 (Grand Rapids: Baker, 1979), 337.
3. Randy Alcorn, *Money, Possessions, and Eternity* (Wheaton, IL: Tyndale, 2003), 43.
4. Erwin W. Lutzer, *Your Eternal Reward: Triumph and Tears at the Judgment Seat of Christ* (Chicago: Moody, 1998), 14. Lutzer also calls his readers to consider that Jesus, who was never selfish, was not only motivated to endure the cross out of obedience to His Father but also for the "joy that was set before him" (Heb. 12:2).
5. For example, see David A. Croteau, "A Biblical and Theological Analysis of Tithing: Toward a Theology of Giving in the New Covenant Era" (PhD diss., Southeastern Baptist Theological Seminary, 2005); and Russell Earl Kelly, *Should the Church Teach Tithing? A Theologian's Conclusions About a Taboo Doctrine* (Lincoln: iUniverse, 2007). Kelly's book is a revised version of his dissertation. See also Stuart Murray, *Beyond Tithing* (Carlisle, UK: Paternoster, 2002). For an old but popular treatment, see John MacArthur Jr., *God's Plan for Giving* (Chicago: Moody, 1982).
6. John MacArthur, *Whose Money Is It Anyway?* (Nashville: Word, 2000), 108.
7. Andrew E. Hill, *Malachi* (New York: Bantam Doubleday, 1998), 44.
8. Ibid.
9. Luke 11:42 could also be included, as it is a parallel account to Matthew 23:23.
10. Andreas J. Köstenberger and David A. Croteau, "'Will a Man Rob God?' (Malachi 3:8): A Study of Tithing in the Old and New Testaments," *Bulletin of Biblical Research* 16, no. 1 (spring 2006): 77–78.
11. A few ministries include T. D. Jakes, Trinity Broadcast Network, Joyce Meyer, Creflo Dollar, Paula White, Benny Hinn, Kenneth Copeland, and Kenneth Hagin. See www.ministrywatch.com to access *Donor Alert Ministries* for 2008 (accessed November 17, 2009).

Scripture Index

Subject Index

A

Abraham, 92–95, 108, 146, 150–51, 178n. 33. *See also* Abram

Abrahamic covenant, 21, 82, 92–94, 102, 178n. 26, 178n. 33

Abram, 150, 178n. 26

Adam, 64, 126, 178n. 26, 180n. 6, 180n. 7, 181n. 8

affirmations, 40, 45, 74

Ahlstrom, Sydney, 32

Alcorn, Randy, 148

atonement, of Christ, 21, 46, 51–52, 70–71, 82–83, 89–92, 102, 178n. 23

attraction, law of, 39–40, 43, 62

authority, 55, 59, 77, 147
  usurp God's, 126

B

Babylonian captivity, 181n. 12

Bakker, Jim, 56

Bakker, Tammy Faye, 55

beliefs, 29–30, 32, 42–43, 57–58, 72
  charismatic, 54
  core, 26, 34, 164
  correct doctrinal, 19
  educated, 88
  incorrect, 20, 81
  professed, 16
  religious, 27

benevolence, 22, 145, 149, 151
  financial, 144
  prorating of, 129

Bible. *See* hermeneutics; suffering, biblical examples of; wealth, biblical teaching on

blessings, 17, 21, 61, 88, 101, 125, 152, 160
  financial, 13–14, 149
  of God, 75, 77, 93–94, 164
  promised unconditional, 78
  spiritual, 94, 149, 158

blood, 77, 119–20

body of Christ, 134, 137, 156

Bolden, Robert, 67–68

Bonhoeffer, Dietrich, 147

Braden, Charles, 32

Bridges, Jerry, 85

Buddha, 32

Burkmar, Lucius, 29

C

Calvin, John, 147

Capps, Charles, 55, 59

Christ. *See* Jesus

Christian charities, 156, 158, 161

Christian Science, 31, 34–35, 51

Christian Stewardship Association, 124

church, 16–17, 27–28, 33, 55, 57, 72, 76, 79, 81, 85, 98, 123–25, 136, 155–59, 161, 163
  early, 109, 137, 154

church councils, 26, 35

Coleman, Simon, 30

Collier, Robert, 45–46

About the Authors

David W. Jones (PhD) serves as Associate Professor of Christian Ethics and Coordinator of ThM and Thesis Studies at Southeastern Baptist Theological Seminary. His doctoral work in the field of financial ethics has been recognized in the *Evangelical Studies Bulletin* for its contribution to scholarship. He has authored or coauthored more than a dozen articles and books over a wide range of moral issues, including *Reforming the Morality of Usury* and *God, Marriage and Family.* Dr. Jones is a frequent speaker at churches, ministries, and Christian conferences. Dr. Jones currently resides in the Raleigh/Durham area of North Carolina with his wife and four children.

Russell S. Woodbridge (PhD) is a former Assistant Professor of Theology and Church History at Southeastern Baptist Theological Seminary and is currently serving in Eastern Europe with the International Mission Board. He has lectured on the prosperity gospel in both the classroom and church, and published articles on Christian stewardship. He has lived overseas in Germany (working), in Austria (church planting), and in Ukraine (teaching). Prior to seminary, Dr. Woodbridge was Vice-President for Equity Derivatives for Salomon Brothers AG in Frankfurt, Germany. Dr. Woodbridge currently resides in Kiev, Ukraine, with his wife and four children.